Computerizing Your Accounting System

All About Integrated Accounting Software

Computerizing Your Accounting System

All About Integrated Accounting Software

One Point™

Hayden Book Company
A DIVISION OF HAYDEN PUBLISHING COMPANY, INC.
HASBROUCK HEIGHTS, NEW JERSEY / BERKELEY, CALIFORNIA

Typesetting:	EPOP Graphic Arts Center
Text Design:	Richard Jantz, Tulpa Productions
Production:	Randy Fontes
Acquisitions Editor:	Therese A. Zak
Cover Design:	Jim Bernard/Peter Tyras

Printed in the United States of America.

1	2	3	4	5	6	7	8	9	
85	86	87	88	89	90	91	92	93	YEAR

Acknowledgments

The research, writing, and production of this book have been a collaborative project involving the efforts of many talented people. One Point gratefully acknowledges the participation of the following writers, editors, researchers, evaluators, and consultants in the preparation of this book.

Principal writers and researchers: Robert Warren, Eric Knorr, Marlene Nesary, and Cynthia Spoor.

One Point Publications and Research Staff: Stevan Cloudtree, President; Jonathan Hathaway, Executive Vice-President; Richard J. Jantz, Director & Senior Editor; Eric Knorr, Associate Editor; Trish Ventura, Assistant Editor; Cindy Fontes, Manager.

Additional editorial and technical support: Bruce Anderson, Anne Beede, Frances M. Christie, Walter J. Clegg, Bill Dempsey, Kathie DeVito, Tom Evans, Jon Fach, Rosemarie E. Falanga, Denyse Forman, Sarada Hopkins, Stephen Ritchie, John Rompel, Balfour Smith, Mike Smith, Paul Stottlemyer, Martha Strizich, and Joni Yamamoto.

Hayden Book Company Computer Science Staff: Michael Violano, Editorial Director; Therese A. Zak, Acquisitions Editor.

Software Evaluators: Dick Andersen, Karen Beaman, Jim Bohannon, Francois Brenot, Noel Carrasco, Peggy Casey, Dan DeSalvo, Dan Ditmars, Shirley Hunt, Ann Longenecker, Brian McCue, Richard L. Mosher, Bill Oakes, John Propst, Alex Veech, and Robert Warren.

A special thanks also is extended to all of the integrated accounting system software publishers and distributors who made copies of their products available for evaluation and review during the completion of this project.

Preface

Every business transaction, from buying capital equipment to clearing a few items of inventory, becomes part of a company's permanent records. "The books" not only contain a business's financial information, but also its reputability. With so much at stake, many accounting professionals have been wary of letting a microcomputer handle their books.

Thanks to today's sophisticated and powerful microcomputer hardware and software, however, a growing number of accounting businesses are converting to computerized accounting. Assured that automated systems follow "Generally Accepted Accounting Principles" and incorporate data security measures, more and more businesspeople are embracing the time- and labor-saving advantages afforded by computerized accounting.

Small to medium-sized businesses and even divisions of large corporations can profit abundantly from the powerful features provided by microcomputer integrated accounting software. A computerized system can make such tasks as entering and posting transactions, performing end-of-period closings, and tracking payables and receivables much more efficient and easily managed. The ready accessibility of financial information in diverse formats is perhaps the biggest attraction of all. The array of up-to-date financial reports available through an automated system is so vast, it may well have a profound effect on how a business is run.

Integrated accounting software refers to a full-function system comprised of the "big five" modules (individual programs) in microcomputer accounting: General Ledger, Accounts Receivable, Accounts Payable, Inventory Control, and Payroll. The ability to integrate these programs means that a single entry can be distributed automatically to several modules, and that the routines used to perform functions throughout the system are largely uniform. Most of the accounting software packages reviewed in this book are comprised of modules that also will perform on their own.

The purpose of this book is to help you choose, from the many systems now on the market, the integrated accounting software package which will be most useful to your business.

Part I, *Integrated Accounting Technology*, introduces the basic features common to most accounting software packages. Part II, *Integrated Accounting Software*, singles out one accounting software system as a model, or "benchmark," product against which other systems can be measured. It also provides reviews of several outstanding or best-selling integrated accounting packages. A series of comprehensive product comparison charts concludes the section. Part III, *Integrated Accounting Resources*, includes a glossary, directory of accounting software products, and a bibliography on materials relating to computerized accounting systems.

More specifically, Chapter 1, *Exploring Computerized Accounting*, takes a look at the advantages of automated accounting, and explains how accounting data is stored and protected. It also covers the basic components of a microcomputer system. Chapter 2, *Operating Automated Accounting*

Systems, examines each module of an integrated accounting system in depth, and concludes with an overview of the process of converting from a manual to an automated system.

Chapter 3, *Charting Your Accounting Needs,* gives you the opportunity to review your business's accounting requirements, and match those needs to the features offered by various accounting software packages. A Needs Assessment Checklist allows you to make a point-by-point comparison of the integrated accounting products reviewed in this book.

In Chapter 4, *Reviewing the Benchmark Product,* an outstanding accounting software package is examined in detail, and used as a standard of comparison against other accounting systems. Chapter 5, *Surveying the Competition,* provides you with reviews and actual evaluations of many of the leading accounting products available today.

Chapter 6, *Comparing Accounting Systems,* is a valuable reference that enables you to compare the products reviewed in the previous chapters by using a series of charts. These charts also are designed to help you fill in the Needs Assessment Checklist in Chapter 3.

The remainder of the book serves as a reference library of further information. The Glossary is divided into two sections: one consisting of general computing terms, and one defining accounting software terminology. Appendix A, *Evaluation and Review Criteria,* is a reproduction of the test instrument used for evaluating the products in Chapter 5. Appendix B, *Investment Software Directory,* is a thorough list of current products. Appendix C, *Bibliography,* offers further references to sources consulted in preparing this book.

Since it's still difficult for many businesses to find someone with expertise in both accounting and microcomputer technologies, you'll probably find that much of the information in this book is quite exclusive. If your knowledge of accounting is minimal, however, it's also advisable to consult with an accountant to ensure that you select a package with the features that best meet your needs.

This book is a product of One Point, a unique distributor of microcomputer products and product information to major corporations and businesses. You may find it valuable to use the One Point™ computer information network for the most up-to-date product information available. To subscribe to this modem-accessible network, contact: One Point, 2835 Mitchell Drive, Walnut Creek, California 94598, or call (800) 222-2250.

Contents

Part I: Integrated Accounting Technology

Part II: Integrated Accounting Software

Part III: Integrated Accounting Resources

Computerizing Your Accounting System

All About Integrated Accounting Software

Part I

Integrated Accounting Technology

Chapter 1

Exploring Computerized Accounting

Every successful business depends on the accuracy, timeliness, and availability of its financial records. If you are a businessperson involved in bookkeeping, budgeting, investing, managing, purchasing, or virtually any other business function, you probably need financial data at your fingertips on a daily basis.

A computerized accounting system can help you streamline all these critical functions, and reduce your operating costs. Automated transaction processing is less time-consuming and more accurate than manual bookkeeping. When key employees are freed from paper work, they can spend more time identifying and planning the most profitable business activities.

The latest generation of accounting management software for low-cost microcomputer hardware has been a boon to small and large businesses alike. These accounting systems usually consist of five major program modules, including: general ledger, accounts receivable, accounts payable, inventory control, and payroll. Some larger systems include even more than these basic five modules.

In this book, the term *integrated accounting software* is used to refer to a computerized accounting system in which separate modules can be linked together to share files or file structures. In most cases, however, these modules also operate in an independent or "stand-alone" capacity, enabling you to build up your system function by function.

In many companies, the entire cost of automation, including personnel training, can be recovered by computerizing just one accounting function. For example, a company with a large inventory could identify slow-moving items with an automated inventory tracking system, and use this information to minimize unnecessary stock on hand. Or, a business with spiraling accounts receivable could use a computerized system to bill its customers with greater speed and accuracy, thus increasing operating capital.

On the other hand, the purchase of a full-service, integrated system has several strong advantages—particularly in terms of the extensive financial reporting capabilities now offered by many accounting packages. Functions formerly performed by an outside accountant on a monthly, quarterly, or yearly basis can be fulfilled in-house by a trained employee using a computerized accounting system. This gives management instant access to the timely, comprehensive financial data necessary for sound business decisions.

Here are but a few of the many functions an integrated accounting system can help you perform:

- Analysis of sales activities
- Preparation of cash requirement reports
- Listing of critical inventory
- Comparison of budgets with actual performance
- Analysis of company profitablity
- Preparation of vendor payment schedules
- Analysis of customer credit liability
- Comparison of employee pay scales
- Cost recovery analysis
- Invoice calculation and printout
- Aging report preparation

This chapter explains the essential features and functions you should understand when selecting an automated accounting system. It discusses how accounting information is stored, and how this information is protected from both error and tampering. Finally, the chapter takes a basic look at the type of computer hardware you'll need.

How Computerized Accounting Works

Automated accounting offers you the luxury of entering transaction information through a keyboard—certainly a more efficient method than transcribing figures onto a columnar pad. But the real advantages of an integrated accounting system lie in what it does with the information you enter. Any or all of the modules in an integrated system may be affected by entering one transaction into a single ledger.

If you post a transaction in accounts receivable, for example, it will be relayed instantly to the general ledger. You may have to enter a brief command into the computer, but you will enter transaction details only once. Since up to 95 percent of the work in accounting involves posting and editing transactions, the automatic distribution offered by integrated software can be a valuable time-saving tool.

For example, say you own a hardware store. Every day, you receive payments from customer purchases. If you post the day's receipts to a cash journal, then post the week's totals onto a trial balance sheet, and finally tally these figures on a monthly basis for the general ledger accounts, you will have processed the same set of cumulative figures three times. An accounts receivable module integrated with a general ledger module could save you two of those three entry tasks. You will not only have freed up valuable personnel time, you will have reduced the opportunities for error. Most integrated packages automatically calculate subtotals and will not post them unless they balance—a further ensurance of data accuracy.

The following sections introduce the general features common to all of the modules in an integrated accounting system. Since reporting capabilities vary from module to module, exploration of the wealth of reports available through computerized accounting may be found in Chapter 2, "Operating Automated Accounting Systems," which covers each module in depth.

Information Storage

An automated accounting system can't do away with all the repetitive tasks associated with accounting. It can, however, store the fundamental information necessary for numerous reports and calculations and use it again and again, without requiring you to enter it more than once. The "global information" common to all functions in an accounting module is referred to as the *company profile.*

The company profile typically contains the company name and address, fiscal periods, interest rates, tax codes, next available check number, and so on. This information is entered when you *install,* or set up, the software to run on your particular computer system. Once the company profile is established, it has global effects throughout the program. In other words, the exact wording in the company profile (e.g., a company's name) often is repeated on all reports, checks, statements, and invoices. Although the actual degree of flexibility varies from program to program, the company profile may be difficult to alter after the information is entered. Therefore, it's crucial to identify all of the company profile data you will need to include before installing the software.

After the company profile, the *master file* contains the information with the most far-reaching effects. The master file is really the nucleus of each accounting module, since it contains the accounts to which all transactions are posted. In the general ledger, the master file is called the *chart of accounts,* the primary list of accounts in an accounting system. In accounts receivable and accounts payable, the master files are the *customer file* and the *vendor file,* respectively. Inventory control centers around the *item file*, and all payroll transactions are posted to the *employee file.* Each account in a master file has its own *account number,* which acts as a reference for all transactions involving that particular account.

Another type of information storage can be found in *transaction files,* which are the main source of historical or audit trail information for an accounting function. They can include records of invoices, payments, adjustments, purchases, shipments, and journal entries. Unlike master files, transaction files are held in the computer system's memory only until an audit trail has been printed, and the totals have been distributed to appropriate accounts. Then, transaction files are purged to make way for new transactions.

Transaction files should be cross-referenced by account number. For example, an invoice in accounts receivable transaction files should contain the necessary details regarding items purchased, date, price, tax, terms, and so forth, as well as the customer account number. Then, when you post accounts receivable transactions, a well-integrated system will sort through and distribute pertinent transaction details to the correct customer account, to the appropriate general ledger accounts, and into your inventory module.

Data Security

Data security presents two main considerations. The first, and most obvious, involves who will be able to access your accounting records, and how you can prevent unauthorized personnel from obtaining those records. The second consideration is the integrity of the data itself, and how it can be safeguarded from a system malfunction or user error.

Most integrated accounting packages come with *password protection,* which guards against unauthorized access to data. Passwords are most often created by the person chiefly responsible for computer operations. In some accounting software systems, entering a single password admits you to every module and every data file. Other systems offer more sophisticated password protection routines.

Multilevel security is desirable when more than one operator uses your system. One employee, for example, can be assigned a password that allows access to only one subsidiary ledger, while a senior staff member alone has the password for the general ledger. Or, a business may have non-accounting personnel who take customer orders over the phone, approving purchase requests on the basis of account information they can access on the computer display screen. Through the multilevel protection in some systems, you could give these employees a password that allows them to view information, but not to change it.

Some accounting programs offer a *key security* system, which relies on a specially encoded floppy disk. Inserting the key disk into the computer's disk drive (explained later in this chapter) admits you to files otherwise inaccessible. Security is then simply an issue of controlling access to the key disk.

New schemes for data protection are being developed all the time; however, there's no such thing as absolute electronic security. Probably the simplest way to defend your data from deliberate tampering or unauthorized perusal is to control access to the computer itself.

Securing the internal integrity of your accounting information is every bit as important as guarding it from outside interference. Some accounting software automatically verifies that your data has been recorded correctly; it also may detect problem areas (i.e., weak spots or faulty sectors) on a disk. This is a highly desirable function, since any problem areas on a disk can be "locked out" once they are identified, keeping your data safe from disk error.

A *backup* disk is by far the best protection against data destruction. Backups are additional reserve copies of your accounting data disks, to ensure against catastrophic errors made by you or your system. Backup copies should be made of all disks containing data you would not want to reconstruct manually. That way, should a power failure or any other serious problem occur during a crucial processing session, you'll have a backup replacement disk handy.

Your Computer System

Since today's microcomputer systems are designed with ease of use in mind, they seldom require professional expertise to set up and connect. To help you understand more about accounting software programs, however, the following section provides a brief orientation on how microcomputers work. For additional information, technical terms (presented in *italics* throughout this book) are also explained in the Glossary. If you require a more comprehensive explanation on microcomputer technology, see the Bibliography (Appendix C) for a list of several excellent references.

As shown in Figure 1-1, a microcomputer system's basic components include: a *system unit,* a *keyboard,* a *monitor,* and *printer.* The system unit houses the electronics that provide a microcomputer's brainpower. It is connected by cables to the keyboard, monitor, and printer, which provide you with data input and output capabilities.

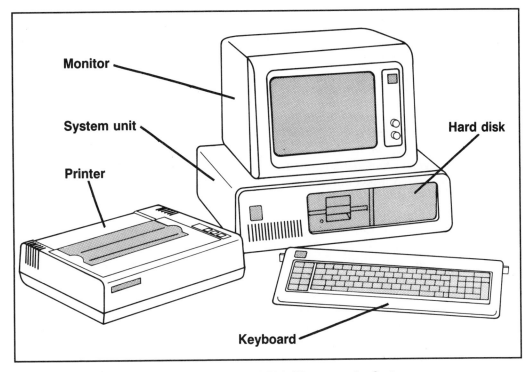

FIGURE 1-1 A Basic Hard Disk Microcomputer System

System Unit

The system unit is the main chassis of the computer system you'll be using. The most important elements within this unit are the *central processing unit (CPU),* the *memory chips,* and one or more *disk drives.*

The CPU acts as a "traffic manager" that controls the flow of data to and from the various components of a computer system. The printed circuit board containing the CPU also holds the microelectronic devices, called "chips," which make up the internal memory of a computer. External memory is provided by the computer system's disk drives, and is explained later in this section.

A microcomputer uses two types of internal memory: *read only memory (ROM)* and *random access memory (RAM)*. ROM consists of a small amount of basic operational data loaded into the memory chips by the manufacturer. It cannot be altered by the user. RAM, on the other hand, is designed to be temporary, and serves as the main memory "workspace" of the computer. When you start up a software program, it is stored in RAM for as long as that program is in operation. As soon as the computer is turned off, the contents loaded into RAM are erased automatically.

In computer terminology, accounting software is said to have a typical "minimum memory requirement" of 128 kilobytes of RAM. A *kilobyte,* abbreviated K, represents 1,024 bytes. A *byte* is equivalent to a single character—i.e., a letter, a number, or a symbol.

The IBM Personal Computer (IBM PC), generally recognized as the most popular microcomputer currently sold, comes from the factory with 128K of RAM—enough to meet the requisite minimum for most stand-alone accounting programs. However, to fully realize the capabilities of full-featured, integrated accounting software, you'll generally need at least two times (256K) or even four times (512K) the memory available on the standard model.

In order to obtain this type of memory capability, you have several options. First, you can expand an IBM PC's RAM to 256K by simply buying additional memory chips and plugging them into the printed circuit board that holds the CPU. Beyond that, you need to purchase plug-in memory expansion boards, designed to fit into slots already built into your system unit. Another option for obtaining increased memory and higher operating speed is to select one of the PC's sister machines, the IBM PC-XT or the IBM PC-AT.

The PC-XT is a popular and powerful hard disk (explained below) version of the original PC; the PC-AT offers two to three times the speed, three times more memory, and up to four times the data storage of the PC-XT. The PC-AT also includes network capabilities—the ability for one computer to orchestrate several terminals and operations at the same time.

All three of the computers mentioned above use disk drives, which are common external memory devices employed by microcomputers. Disk drives "play" a disk containing electromagnetic information in much the same way a turntable plays a record. A mechanism similar to a tape recording head, called the *read/write head,* accesses or records data on various sectors of the disk according to instructions received from the software in use. Information on disk, unlike information in RAM, remains intact after the computer is turned off. Disks therefore act as the primary repository for your accounting information.

The disks usually associated with microcomputers are 5¼-inch *floppy disks,* which are physically inserted into the disk drive. Floppy disks contain the flexible electromagnetic medium on which various data is stored. Microcomputer software is "loaded" on floppy disks; when a floppy disk contains software, it is referred to as a *program disk.* The standard IBM PC comes with two disk drives—usually the minimum number for running accounting programs. Normally, one disk drive is used to run the program disk, while the other runs the blank *data disk* on which you will store your own accounting records.

The IBM PC-XT and PC-AT each contain a single disk drive, plus a *hard disk,* also called a "fixed disk" because it is sealed into its own drive. Compared to a standard disk drive, a hard disk can store much more information, can access data approximately 10 times faster, and is more dependable and less vulnerable to accidental loss of data. Hard disks are generally used to store program information, which is transferred onto the hard disk by loading it from the program disk using the standard disk drive. Once this transfer is completed, the standard disk drive is free to run a data disk.

The amount of program data contained in an integrated accounting software package is usually larger than the average microcomputer program. For this reason, the enhanced capabilities of a hard disk are required for some accounting packages, and are recommended for many others. In any case, if you plan on both a fully integrated system and large data files, you should consider a hard disk computer.

Input/Output Devices

As shown in the foreground in Figure 1-1, a keyboard provides the primary vehicle for data input and for executing the various commands that control the computer's functions. Most computer keyboards look like standard typewriter keyboards, with additional keys designated for special functions. The IBM PC keyboard is flanked on the right by a numeric keypad, and on the left by a set of special function keys that perform specific operations assigned by the software program in use.

The remaining two components, the *monitor* and the *printer,* are both output devices. The monitor, technically called a *cathode ray tube (CRT),* is a small television-like device that visually displays data. It's a vital component, and when you select one, you should keep two important considerations in mind. First is the monitor's *resolution*, or image sharpness capability. The higher the monitor's resolution, the less a user will be subject to eyestrain or to misreading the onscreen information.

The second consideration is whether you want a color or monochrome (single-color) monitor. A monochrome monitor is adequate for most applications—accounting software, for instance, seldom makes extensive use of color variation. However, some accounting packages allow you to display information from different modules on the same screen simultaneously, and use color to distinguish between information groups. If you are considering an integrated accounting package that relies heavily on this ability, a color monitor would be a well-advised purchase.

Output also is provided via the printer, which produces printed pages called *hardcopy.* Since printed financial reports are one of the most important aspects of automated accounting, it's imperative to select a printer that can generate clean and easy-to-read hardcopy.

Printers come in many sizes, run at different speeds, and print in different type styles and column widths. Since most accounting software requires printers with 132-column capability, you'll need to check the minimum number of columns specified by the software you are considering.

The standard printer for computerized accounting is the *dot matrix printer,* which produces characters by composing dot patterns on paper. Dot matrix printers are economical, reasonably fast, and usually offer graphics capability. Another type of printer is the *letter quality printer,* which is slower and more expensive than a dot matrix printer, but generates output that looks professionally typed. Because automated accounting demands large amounts of hardcopy, most users prefer the dot matrix printer's higher operating speed.

In conclusion, one final point should be emphasized. Most experienced users agree that it's better to purchase a minimal version of a powerful computer system than to buy the full-blown version of a limited system. Then, as your accounting business grows and as more advanced business software becomes available, you'll be able to expand your current system to meet any increasing speed or memory capacity demands.

Chapter 2

Operating Automated Accounting Systems

❖ If you understand accounting, then you already have a sound basis for learning how an automated accounting system works. Generally Accepted Accounting Procedures provide the parameters for accounting programs, and these rules govern processing of your financial information. The main difference between a manual and a computerized system is the increased efficiency with which a computer stores and retrieves your accounting data.

A computerized system stores your data in *files,* which are collections of related information saved on disk. Each file is comprised of subdivisions called *records*. The customer file in accounts receivable, for example, is made up of individual records, each of which contains all information on a specific customer.

When you enter information into a record, you do so through an *input screen*, also called a "video form." An input screen is an electronic version of a paper form, divided into different areas called *fields*. Each field is designed to hold a specific type of information. An input screen for an invoice, for example, has one field for the date, one for the customer name, one for the amount, and so on. When these fields are filled in by typing entries on the keyboard, the computer adds this information to the overall record for that customer.

Although an automated system performs such day-to-day entry tasks far more efficiently than a manual one, its most remarkable benefit resides in its financial reporting capability. Fast, efficient retrieval of specific accounting records is epitomized by one of the latest developments in accounting software, the *query system*. If you want to know the status of a customer or vendor account, an inventory item, or even an employee, a query system will retrieve this information instantly in summary form and display it on your computer's monitor.

Businesses that take most of their orders over the phone often use a query system to check the status of an account while the customer is still on the line. If the system is integrated with an inventory control module, the operator can check stock availability as well.

Like a manual system, a computerized accounting system relies on journal listings to provide the audit trail necessary for sound business practice. Each module in an integrated accounting system prints out journal listings after posting or distributing transactions. Most accounting systems require you to print a daily journal before anything else can be done with the day's transactions, thus ensuring the "purity" of the audit trail. More sophisticated routines will record the password ID of the person using the system when a particular transaction is posted or journal produced.

This chapter examines the various procedures involved in running a computerized accounting system, from setting up the master file to generating analytical reports. A separate section is devoted to each of the five modules highlighted in this book, and each section covers the features relating to specific accounting applications.

Before setting up a computerized accounting system, however, you should carefully study the rhythm and structure of your current fiscal cycle. Then research as many accounting software packages as possible, using the Needs Assessment Checklist in Chapter 3, to help you prioritize your requirements and compare software products feature by feature.

General Ledger

The general ledger (G/L) is the nucleus of any accounting system. It reflects all financial activity within an entire company. Even a 50-cent handling charge has a net effect as both a debit and a credit in at least two general ledger accounts.

As illustrated in Figure 2-1, G/L activities can be grouped into three major areas: *transaction processing, posting,* and *financial reporting*. In addition to receiving manually entered data, a general ledger that is part of an integrated accounting system will receive the majority of its transaction information in the form of summaries from other modules. This information is posted to G/L accounts during end-of-month processing.

Since the general ledger is the central storehouse for your accounting data, it's also the logical place to consolidate that information and arrange it in the form of financial reports. The financial reporting function of your G/L package is your main source of information concerning your company's status.

The Master File

The flow of activity in Figure 2-1 is directed and defined by the chart of accounts, the general ledger's master file. The accounts listed in this master file are divided into the three categories fundamental to accounting: balance sheet accounts, income/expense accounts, and retained earnings.

A user-defined numbering system provides the vehicle for constructing the chart of accounts. A typical G/L package will offer a numbering scheme that allows you to assign account numbers from five digits to 12 digits long. In most systems, the first character represents the account type. A common grouping might be as follows:

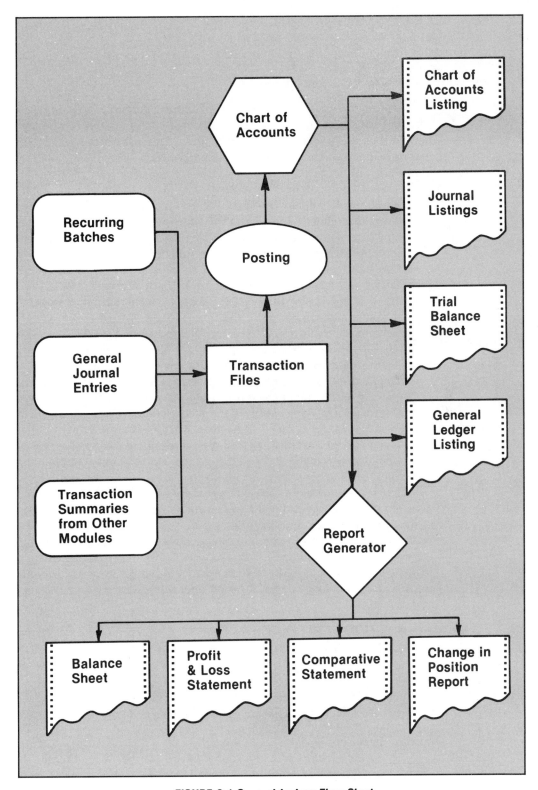

FIGURE 2-1 General Ledger Flow Chart

- 100000—199999 Assets
- 200000—299999 Liabilities
- 300000—399999 Equity
- 400000—499999 Income
- 500000—599999 Expenses

Some G/L software comes with fixed numeric ranges for account types. Although you can't alter these ranges, they shouldn't limit your account-handling ability under most circumstances. However, businesses with unique demands—such as nonprofit organizations—may wish to purchase a more flexible system.

A small company may have 50-80 accounts in its chart of accounts, while a mid-sized company with profit centers (i.e., departments) may have many times that number. If your general ledger will be tracking transactions according to profit center, you must be able to include some form of departmental identification within the account number itself.

The most common way of handling departments is to append a separate (usually alphabetic) identifier to the basic account number. For example, in a small company with five separate retail departments, retail sales accounts might be coded as follows: I4010A, I4010B, I4010C, etc. Some accounting packages may require a three-digit code at the end, such as I4010-100, I4010-105, and so on. This account number design feature allows you to sort information by department on financial reports.

The method by which an accounting package's chart of accounts is *justified* (aligned by either the left or right margin) may affect its sorting and reporting order. For example, if the account numbers are left-justified, Account 1011 would come after Account 101, and before Account 102. If the codes are right-justified, all four-digit account numbers would follow three-digit account numbers. You can get around this potential dilemma by setting up all account numbers with the same number of digits.

The sequence you set up on the chart of accounts is, by default, the same sequence that appears in the trial balance worksheet, in the G/L listing, in the journal listings, and (in some systems) on financial reports. If you want a profit and loss statement to have accounts listed in a particular sequence, the accounts must be in that same order on the chart of accounts. In some schemes, an additional field is provided in the chart of accounts to place accounts in a certain order on financial reports—a useful, time-saving feature.

Transaction Processing

Ninety percent of the work performed in an accounting system involves transaction processing. This is where the real labor-saving and increased accuracy of a computerized system show their strength.

Typically, transactions are handled in *batches*, which are groups of entries related by date or type. For instance, all of the orders processed in one day, or all of the vendor invoices paid during the week, might be entered, balanced, and posted as a batch.

The *general journal* is one source of transaction information. The entries in this journal are made directly into the general ledger, and are not funneled through any other accounting module. A general journal contains transactions that are not easily categorized, such as those that occur in another fiscal cycle.

Recurring batches are another type of input. These are transactions that occur on a monthly basis, such as fixed asset depreciation. The recurring batch function will allow you to amortize these expenses into monthly amounts, and automatically charge them against the appropriate G/L account.

In an integrated system, the bulk of input to the general ledger comes from the day-to-day transactions entered into other modules. This input comes in the form of transaction summaries, transferred to the appropriate G/L accounts during end-of-month processing.

Posting

After transactions have been entered and checked for accuracy, they are posted to their G/L accounts. The posting function sorts transactions by account number order, then merges them with transactions already posted. A general ledger should provide three basic types of posting: normal, special, and end-of-year.

Normal posting is the assignment of transactions to their designated account in the general ledger. This procedure usually is performed on transactions that occur during the current fiscal period, and always is performed on transactions occurring within the current fiscal year.

Special posting is the assignment of transactions from the prior fiscal year. Categories such as depreciation and inventory adjustments often require posting after the end of the year, so the ability to enter and post after closing is clearly a necessity.

End-of-year posting is the process of closing the general ledger for the fiscal year. When called upon to perform this function, an automated general ledger calculates the year-to-date profit or loss from the income and expense accounts, and posts that amount to the retained earnings account. End-of-year processing also clears the income and expense accounts for the current 12 months, sets these amounts into the historical account data area, and brings forward account balances to start the new fiscal year.

General Ledger Outputs

G/L modules usually produce two kinds of output: listings and reports. *Listings* are basic auditing and editing documents that are printed out by the program in a fixed format. *Reports*, on the other hand, often can be customized to fit your reporting requirements, and provide the most useful financial information regarding your business.

The three most common G/L listings are:

- Chart of accounts listing
- Trial balance sheet
- General ledger listing

The chart of accounts listing provides a handy reference when posting transactions. It's a simple listing of all G/L accounts, showing the account name, number, and type.

A trial balance sheet is a running summary of G/L activity. This listing shows only the balance on each account, divided into debit and credit columns. It acts as a worksheet, and you should be able to print it out at any time.

A general ledger listing shows all transactions made to general ledger accounts. It lists dates, descriptions, source codes, and fiscal posting periods.

G/L modules differ widely in their ability to generate reports. Some will offer as many as 100 different formats built into the package. Some will offer only the bare minimum listing capability, and will require you to design any further analytical reports you need.

Some of the more common uses for a report generator include the following:

- Balance sheet
- Profit and loss statement
- Comparative statement
- Change in financial position report

A balance sheet is one of the most basic accounting documents. It shows a company's financial position in fundamental terms: assets, liabilities, and equity. G/L accounts may be arranged in the account number order you prefer, and broken down by cost center if applicable.

Profit and loss statements allow detailing of user-selected accounts, in the order you designate. Normally, subtotals for gross income, selling and administrative expenses, gross profit, and net profit should be available.

Reports designed to facilitate comparative analysis, such as those that contrast budgets to actual performance, are called comparative statements. In a manual system, comparative statements often require extensive research into past performance and numerous calculations. A computerized system can perform these tasks in a matter of minutes.

A change in financial position report may measure the extent to which your business has altered across any given period. This report most commonly measures change from the beginning to the end of a year.

In some packages, the custom report generator is flexible and sophisticated, offering the ability to compare financial information from prior accounting periods, including the previous year. Once you've installed your accounting system, the variety of reports available is often one of the most useful aspects of computerized accounting. Financial reporting capabilities therefore may be your singlemost important consideration when choosing a G/L package.

Accounts Receivable

Many managers feel they have more to gain from computerizing their accounts receivable (A/R) operations than any other aspect of their business. Instant access to customer information, keeping track of discounts and late charges, and invoicing without delay can give you an idea of when to expect payment from specific customers, and help you time your billing cycle to enhance your cash flow.

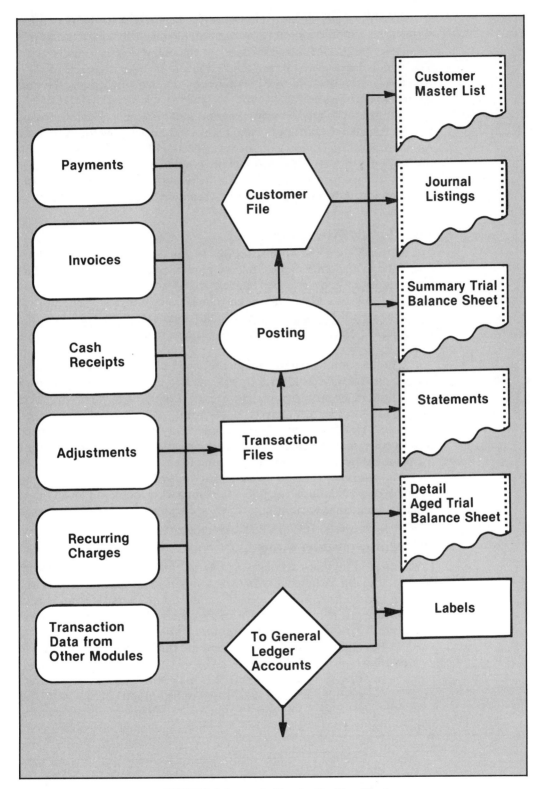

FIGURE 2-2 Accounts Receivable Flow Chart

The A/R cycle, illustrated in Figure 2-2, begins with the input of transaction information. This information is entered manually by data entry personnel, or by the A/R program itself, if the entry is a recurring charge. Transaction data also may be acquired automatically from a separate module, which records both customer and inventory item information at the time an order is processed.

At the end of the accounting period, your program should calculate any interest charges and apply them to the total amount due for the period. An A/R program generates statements, collects and consolidates G/L information, purges open item accounts of completed transactions, and summarizes balance forward accounts for the period. Along the way, you can examine your A/R module's activities through a variety of useful listings and reports.

The Master File

The customer list is the A/R master file. It contains data fields for such information as customer name, address, phone, credit limit, terms, contact person, sales tax code, salesperson, year-to-date totals, and comments. You should be able to add and delete customers, and change any or all of the customer details. If you set credit limits and/or discount amounts in a customer file, for instance, a good A/R package will let you override those limits.

The customer account numbering system used by the program is another important consideration. For small companies, a simple four- or five-digit number may be sufficient. Larger companies may require tracking of customers by salesperson, department, or location, and a longer, segmented, alphanumeric account number may be required. If you need reports concentrating on these classifications, the capability for generating them should be available in the A/R module.

The customer list is so valuable that you will want to print it out on a regular basis, as well as carefully maintain backup copies on disk. In the unlikely event of a system failure, your backups will ensure that your customer list can be reconstructed without missing an account.

Transaction Processing

Payments and invoices account for the bulk of transaction information entered into the A/R ledger. Data entry personnel most often charge customer accounts from invoice copies, and apply payment from checks or cash receipts. However, an A/R module may also collect information electronically from *order entry* or *point-of-sale* programs.

With some accounting software systems, the ability to record and process customer orders and generate invoices is included within the A/R module. In other systems, these activities may be consigned to a separate order entry module, or to an inventory control module (explained later in this chapter). The order entry module consolidates customer account information and sends it along to A/R, while simultaneously collecting information on items sold and transferring it to inventory. Order entry applications handle a variety of customer accounts, wholesale or retail, large or small.

Point-of-sale technology, on the other hand, generally caters to retail trade. Point-of-sale features can be quite elaborate, with computer terminals doubling as virtual cash registers at the retail outlet. The details of a transaction are input at the time of sale, fed into an inventory tracking module, a customer account file, and a G/L control account, and then an invoice is printed on the spot. If the retail outlet is connected by modem to a main office, the day's transactions can be transmitted over the phone that night, helping to maximize the efficiency of business operations.

The remaining types of input are handled within the A/R package exclusively. Adjustments are especially important to accommodate properly. There should be enough blank fields to record adequate detail, so the nature of the adjustment can be reconstructed by an auditor.

After receiving input via direct entry or from another module, an A/R package processes transactions in relation to customer accounts. There are two methods for processing receivables transactions: open item and balance forward.

In *open item* processing, all customer sales for a given fiscal period are invoiced and applied separately. Each of these purchases has its own invoice and reference number, and appears as a separate item on the monthly statement. Detail for an open item account is maintained from period to period until each invoice is paid in full. If a customer pays certain invoices and holds others, these specifics are accurately represented on the monthly statement.

In *balance forward* accounting, sales are handled as a period total, even though the invoice details (e.g., date, amount, items, etc.) are spelled out on the monthly statement. When payment is received, however, it is applied to the account total, and the balance remaining is carried forward into the next period. All other information is cleared from the record to make way for new transactions during end-of-month processing.

Another kind of balance forward account is a *revolving charge* account. In this case, the system condenses invoicing detail into an outstanding balance, and calculates the amount due for each period according to the terms established for that customer's account. The amount due is usually a combination of the minimum monthly payment and a percentage of the outstanding balance.

An efficient A/R package will allow you to handle both open item and balance forward accounts simultaneously, and let you switch accounts from one type to the other as needed. Since open item accounts contain much more data, they will require a proportionately larger amount of disk space.

Recurring charges may take the form of a monthly payment or of a contract amount payable per month. A special control account generally is set up to oversee such changes prior to actual posting. The control account would include information such as the total amount to be paid over time, the periodic amount, and the number of payments or postings required. Payment history also might be fed back into this account.

Interest is a form of posting as well as a form of input. The interest due is calculated by the program and posted automatically to the customer account. The amount of interest charged can be specified in the master file for each customer, but, as previously mentioned, it's best to select a package that will let you change the amount without much difficulty. The date after which interest on a purchase accrues also is specified in the master file, and should allow subsequent change.

If a G/L module is in place, the end-of-period functions will include a consolidation into G/L account numbers, a sort into account number order, at least one forced audit/edit listing, and an automatic distribution of corrected details into the general ledger itself. Since some A/R packages will not function without a G/L chart of accounts located elsewhere in an integrated system, make certain you select a stand-alone program if your immediate objective is to automate accounts receivable only.

Accounts Receivable Output

A good A/R module can help with customer account maintenance and with cash flow management. It does this chiefly through listing and reporting capabilities. The following items include several useful A/R outputs:

- Customer master list
- Detail aged trial balance
- Summary aged trial balance
- Statements
- Mailing labels

The customer master list is merely a printout of your customer file. Generally, you can sort customer accounts in either alphabetical or account number order. This information seldom is consolidated in any other report, so it's imperative to have a current printout of customer statistics on hand for easy reference. An A/R module that allows you to sort customers by such criteria as salesperson or credit terms is an excellent tool for marketing analysis.

The detail aged trial balance sheet is the most consulted report generated by the A/R module. Detail for each account is shown in account number order, with every transaction listed in one of a series of columns according to its age. The purpose of this report is to reflect the totals of each "aged" column, as well as the grand total of accounts receivable, so that cash flow projection is not only possible but reasonably accurate. Nearly all A/R packages support standard 30/60/90-day aging periods represented by their respective columns. Businesses with more unique requirements, however, may need a program with user-definable aging periods as well.

The summary aged trial balance sheet is similar in intent to the detail aged report, but without the transaction detail. Some companies prefer to consult the summary report for cash flow analysis, others prefer the detailed report. A proficient A/R module offers both at any time in the fiscal period.

Once all monthly activity is entered and posted, you can complete the accounting cycle by generating customer statements. Some systems provide a fixed format only, designed for a particular brand of blank statement form, while others allow customization. If you are considering a system with fixed statements, study the form and make sure it supplies the information with which you and your customers are comfortable.

Many A/R packages will print out mailing labels based on your customer file. This is useful for mailings to preferred customers, price list announcements, or letters to overdue accounts.

Accounts Payable

Nobody likes paying bills, but putting it off until the last minute can cost you more than the bills themselves. You can lose substantial discounts offered for prompt payment, and, if you wait long enough, you can lose your good credit standing. Computerizing your accounts payable (A/P) activities can help you synchronize bill-paying tasks to your best advantage.

Many companies deal with a multitude of vendors, each offering a variety of discounts and terms. Trying to track these variables by hand can cost you more in labor than it saves in cost of goods. A computerized A/P package can point you toward the best prices, and also help you juggle your check balance, cash flow, discount rates, and overhead account spreads. It will recommend a sequence and timeframe for payments due that maximizes your cash on hand.

The Master File

As shown in Figure 2-3, the master file for accounts payable is the vendor file. This list of repeatedly used suppliers details essentially the same information as the customer list in accounts receivable, with the addition of payment, terms, and discount information.

Unless your business has unique vendor requirements, most A/P modules will give you enough options to approximate your current terms for payables. Check the entry screen for vendor accounts and verify that it will accommodate an adequate number of information fields. Some programs supply sample input forms to expedite the collection and entry of vendor data.

As with any master file, you should be able to add and delete accounts at will, as well as modify any details for a particular vendor. To accomplish this easily, you'll need an A/P module that offers basic keyboard editing functions. Whenever a vendor changes its address, or other essential information, you can access the master file and type in the necessary adjustments.

In looking at various A/P programs, make certain you investigate the limits for the vendor file size. You may need to add memory capacity to your hardware system to get all of your vendor accounts into the system. Or, if you handle your accounts payable as open items, you may need to allocate more memory per account.

Transaction Processing

Invoices are the primary source of transaction information for the A/P ledger. An input screen for invoice data has fields for such standard information as transaction date, vendor account number, description, and so forth. Unlike manual processing, however, you also assign a terms code and G/L account distribution.

As in accounts receivable, the input screen for adjustments should be flexible enough to handle virtually any transaction or correction that can't

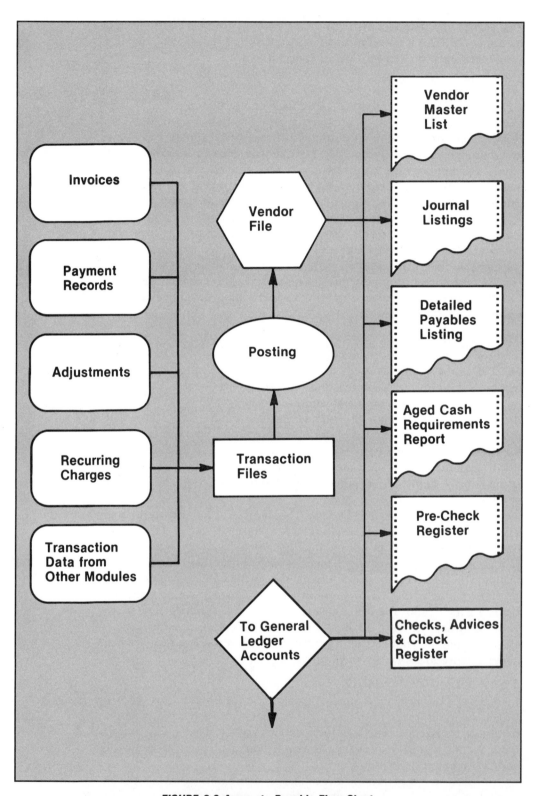

FIGURE 2-3 Accounts Payable Flow Chart

be handled as a standard entry. Through this function you might process write-offs, correct prior mistakes through offsetting entries, or redistribute a transaction to a different G/L account.

Payments to a vendor are not only an output function (a check written to satisfy an invoice received), but also involve an input into specific vendor accounts. Checks that are generated manually outside the computerized system need to be applied to an account within the system.

Checks also may be generated automatically by the system in response to recurring charges. This could be a monthly maintenance fee in your lease agreement, or loan payments to a mortgage house at fixed amounts. A special set of information—global for contracts and payment situations—is installed for these accounts. It acts as a template to print out a check when a recurring charge is due.

In addition, most A/P software allows you to make payments without having to set up a separate vendor account at all. If you make a one-time purchase from a source you are unlikely to use again, the package lets you tie the transaction to a "miscellaneous" account. An account number is assigned temporarily, so the transaction details can be figured into all reports, but you produce the check manually.

After you've entered a batch of invoices and/or adjustments, you should print a listing and examine it for errors. Once it's free of errors and you have a clean printout for auditing, you can post transactions to their appropriate vendor accounts. You may process and post several batches of transactions per accounting period, or you may produce a pre-check register and cash requirements report after only one batch.

At this stage in processing, the program selects the payment arrangement that reflects the discount terms and dates appropriate to each account. If you wish, most programs will let you override established payment terms.

Accounts Payable Outputs

The following group of outputs are indispensable to accounts payable operations:

- Vendor master list
- Detailed payables listing
- Overdue payables listing
- Cash requirements report
- Pre-check register
- Checks, advices, and registers

Printing out the vendor master list at least once every accounting period is just as important as regularly generating a customer master list in A/R. This is not only to satisfy reference and backup requirements. Collecting basic vendor statistics on a single document can give you a quick assessment of your purchasing behavior, and help you decide where to scrutinize your expenses in greater depth.

The detailed payables listing shows all outstanding transaction detail for each vendor account, including invoice number, date received, date due, and so on. For each invoice listed, the report should include any checks and adjustments issued. This report is especially useful for sorting through the particulars of a disputed invoice.

Probably the least pleasant document to examine is the overdue payables listing. You can list overdue payables by vendor or by due date, with the oldest invoice first. Usually, this listing includes vendor terms, allowing you to track late charges and evaluate your standing from vendor to vendor.

The aged cash requirements report—like its counterpart in A/R, the detail aged trial balance—is probably the most consulted report generated by the A/P module. It lists all outstanding invoices, generally in order by vendor account number. Most aged cash requirements reports use the common 30/60/90-day arrangement, and some also allow you to define your own aging periods.

The pre-check register is another often-read document. When you select the criteria of a payment schedule based on A/P reports, the pre-check register will list the invoices that meet those criteria. Then, the majority of A/P packages will let you edit this list, or cancel the series altogether and come up with an entirely different set of payment parameters.

Processing checks and advices are straightforward within most systems, once you select the payments to be made. Most often, you are given the opportunity to set the run date, the sequence of vendors, and the beginning check number. The check register provides the primary A/P audit trail.

If a payroll program's check printing format is fixed, make certain you can easily and cheaply obtain check blanks that match that format. Checks that come as a continuous form can be cut the fastest, but they may require a special printer attachment.

Inventory Control

For many businesses, inventory is the number one asset. Whether you have a high or low volume of items in inventory, tracking those items can be one of your most difficult accounting tasks.

Fast-growing businesses need effective management of items steadily increasing in volume and variety. The enhanced control offered by automation can cut down on the number of inconvenient, impromptu physical inventories you may have to perform, and decrease the likelihood of understocking or overstocking.

Once your inventory control system is in place, you can track sales automatically, item by item, and use this information to determine which articles are slow moving, and which need to be ordered more frequently. Over time, close study of your inventory reports can help you anticipate demand, letting you match stock levels with predicted customer needs.

It's probably fair to say that no accounting software varies as much from package to package as does inventory control. There are three basic types of inventory software: retail, wholesale, and manufacturing. Generally, these are not interchangeable. Therefore, if you think that inventory control is the most important task for your computerized system, you may wish to investigate the inventory module before any other accounting application.

There are four basic costing methods for determining the current value of your inventory: moving average; FIFO (first in, first out); LIFO (last in, first out); and specific identification. Most inventory control software will support at least one or two of these. Once you choose the costing method, however, you can't change it within the same fiscal year.

Figure 2-4 shows the relationship between input and output in an inventory control system. Transaction information comes from both customer and vendor orders, and reports deal with both stocking information and sales analysis. The wealth of information handled by an inventory package tends to make the program itself larger than other modules, and sometimes more expensive as well.

The Master File

The master file for inventory control is the item file. Each item record within the file contains such information as the vendor source, markup factor, year-to-date sales, and so on. While it's a good idea to purchase a system that will hold plenty of item detail, it's also advisable to find one that allows you to bypass any data entry steps that are irrelevant to your business practices.

Most inventory control packages let you establish as many item types as your business requires, or should need in the future. Some also provide departmental identifiers in the item number for handling individual profit centers within a large business. The most versatile item numbering systems handle alphanumeric characters, allow segmentation within the account number structure, and support either vendor numbers from your A/P package, or those assigned within the inventory module itself.

Some businesses require more flexibility in establishing the way items are bought and sold. For instance, you may buy wallpaper from a manufacturer by lot, and sell it by the foot or roll. Therefore, you may need an accounting system that can handle both ways of measuring "quantity sold."

Transaction Processing

A variety of sources provide the transaction information processed by an inventory control package. Most data on incoming inventory items originates from purchase orders and packing slips. Some integrated accounting systems generate purchase orders from a separate module; others cut them within the inventory system itself. Most systems let you enter information, send a copy to the printer, and post changes in inventory levels to the master file on an item-by-item basis. This helps you keep tabs on the overall picture of what's on order and when it's expected to arrive.

As shipments from suppliers arrive, shipping personnel check goods received against the packing slips, and pass them on to data entry personnel. When quantities, types, and costs of goods are entered, and back orders accounted for, the quantity on hand and unit costs on appropriate inventory records are up-to-date. In an integrated system, this information is passed on to the A/P module and consolidated for posting to costing accounts in the G/L module.

When goods are shipped or sold from inventory, customer orders and receipts provide the quantity and sales values to be collected and posted

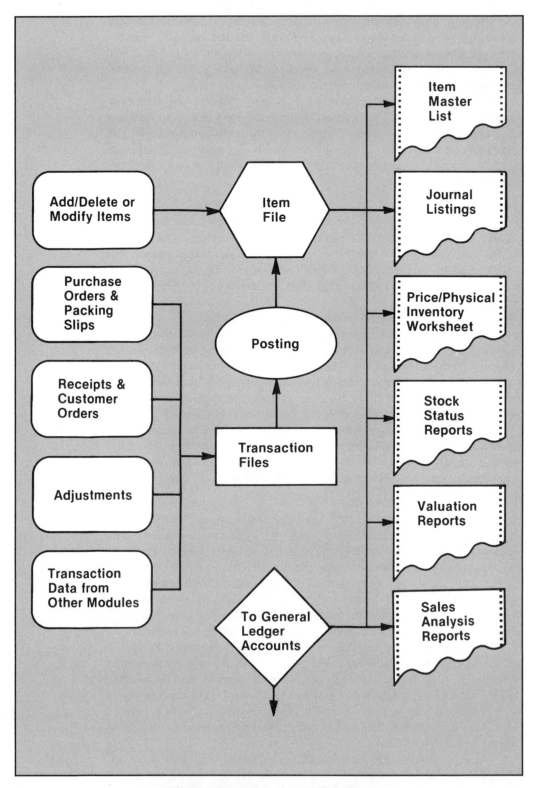

FIGURE 2-4 Inventory Control Flow Chart

to the appropriate item files. This information also affects sales history, generates costing entries for the general ledger, and ties into the operation of accounts receivable.

Adding, deleting, and modifying items is mostly a maintenance function. If you add a new item to your stock, or sell off all of an item and decide not to reorder it, or decide to revise the price or refine the description of an item, you would do so by direct entry into the inventory item file.

Adjustments, as in every other module, are those transactions which cannot be easily classified. In an inventory control system, you might need the adjustments feature when inventory records and physical inventory count do not match, when you dispute an invoice from a supplier for goods not received, or when you need to switch suppliers and cancel items already on order.

Inventory control systems often are integrated with purchase order and/or order entry modules—although some inventory modules may have these functions within their own software. A package with order entry features generates invoices for customers ordering stock items, and may generate shipping documents, credit and adjustment memos, and so on. An inventory module with purchase order capabilities may generate orders automatically when stock on hand falls below certain levels, may pick vendor information from and post charges to accounts payable, and may perform verification routines when shipments are received.

When integrated with a point-of-sale system, an inventory control package can update stock level information immediately. Even large merchandisers can find out their current sales, profits, and stock-on-hand figures at the close of each business day.

Inventory Control Outputs

Some of the more valuable listing and reporting capabilities to look for in a system include the following:

- Category listing
- Stock status report
- Reorder report
- Item valuation report
- Slow-moving items report
- Price/physical inventory worksheet
- Activity reports
- Sales and margin analysis reports
- Bin/shelf labels

A category listing shows all category codes and a brief description of what those codes represent. It also indicates the G/L accounts affected by individual item categories.

When you need a detailed listing of actual inventory, you can print out a stock status report. Items on this report may be sorted by part number, by total on hand, by total on order, or by location.

A reorder report shows which items are low in stock by vendor or a group of vendors, and both the quantity on hand and on order. According to the minimum and maximum limits you've set in the item file, it also may recommend the amount to be reordered. The item valuation report informs you of the value of a single item or group of items in inventory. The value is based on actual cost, selling price, most recent cost, and costing method.

If you're looking for a place to cut your inventory, a slow-moving items report can help identify items that haven't been selling. Inventory packages that allow user-defined parameters for each item (e.g., no sales for 15 days, or sales of less than 15 units in 15 days) are particularly useful in determining which items are of marginal benefit to your business.

A price/physical inventory worksheet assists stock personnel when it's time to match your records with actual stock on hand, and to verify that prices are marked correctly. Programs that allow you to define item category order (i.e., by item number, by warehouse location, or by price structure) make it easier to print listings that reflect the order of items on your shelves.

Activity reports list sales, returns, and receipts along with associated dates, profit margins, and sales volumes. These reports can be an excellent management tool for analyzing trends and planning stocking strategies.

Sales and margin analysis reports are crucial to setting prices and maximizing profits. The more flexible the format for these reports, the better. Generally, inventory control packages will sort item sales by period, by category subtotal, by sales units, by dollars, and by gross profit percentages. More sophisticated programs will print reports that sum up profit gains on an item-by-item basis and calculate gross profit margins.

Bin/shelf labels are a must in a warehouse setting. Using system-generated labels ensures accurate stock pulls and provides an exact match between packing lists and inventory codes.

Payroll

Payroll can be the simplest and most immediately rewarding accounting function to automate. If you do job-costing, or spread administrative salaries over several accounts, a good payroll module will pay for itself, easily and quickly, in saved bookkeeping time—even in a small business.

The conversion to an automated payroll can be quick for your company if you have a small number of employees, and if the payroll function is converted at the beginning of a fiscal year. A company with, say, 20 salaried employees, who all receive their checks at the same time and with the same frequency, should be able to generate automatic checks within the first month.

Payroll modules are generally more expensive than other programs in an accounting software series. This is due to the tax tables accompanying payroll modules. Tax tables take up lots of disk and program space, and require updating at least once a year—sometimes more often. One of the first things you'll want to know about a particular payroll program is how it handles tax table updates (more on this later).

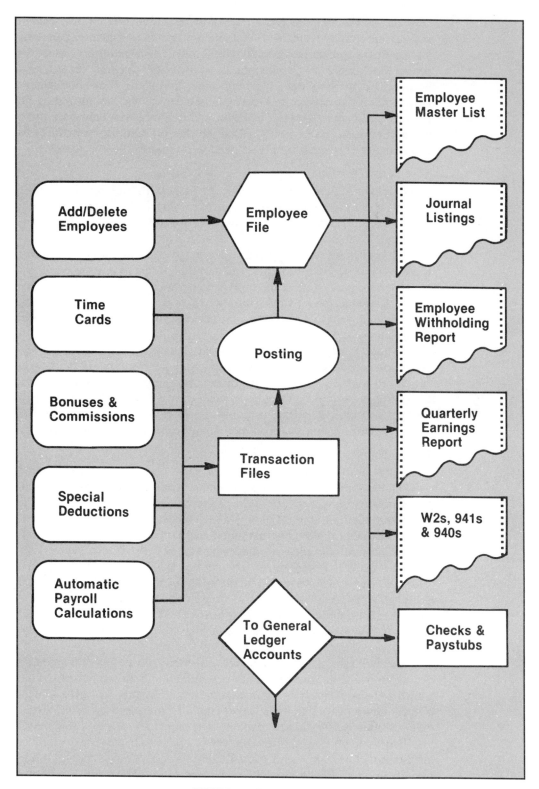

FIGURE 2-5 Payroll Flow Chart

As shown in Figure 2-5, a payroll program receives input regarding monies due employees from several sources, applies pertinent calculations, and produces appropriate payroll checks and deduction reports. Since the proper functioning of a payroll module is so crucial—accurate records must be provided for employees, management, and state, local, and federal governments—the program must be kept current. The key to finding the right payroll system for your business is finding one that helps you maintain accuracy, allows easy edit of changing factors, and provides the exact and complete categorization you need in its master file.

The Master File

The employees' file is the master file for payroll. In looking over various payroll programs, find the total number of employees the system can handle at one time, and also find the total number of deduction categories for any given employee on file.

Most systems will support a variety of pay periods including hourly, weekly, biweekly, semimonthly, and monthly. If you have workers whose rates are calculated by other methods (e.g., piecework, incentive pay, or—as in some manufacturing plants—rates which depend on the cost of finished goods), you'll want to make certain any package you consider can be tailored to meet these special needs.

A good master file for payroll is one that supports the payment and deduction categories you now use, and handles the number of employees you have or anticipate having in the next few years. It also should allow some user-definition of categories, offer easy edit and default override features, and allow department coding and distribution of payroll expenses across as many accounts as required by your current accounting methods.

Tax Tables

A computerized payroll system uses the same tax tables as those used in a manual system, and it must produce the same documentation for appropriate government agencies. Most computerized payroll systems use the annualized method of withholding taxes, since it offers the most coherent way to handle complex, fluctuating tax table relationships. In addition, it only requires one complete set of tax tables to accommodate all pay periods.

In a manual system, gross pay can be calculated for anything from hourly to yearly pay periods. The tax table for that particular pay period is applied to produce net pay. In a computerized system, the gross pay is multiplied by the number of periods in a year. If your employees are paid weekly, their gross weekly pay would be multiplied by 52. If paid biweekly, gross pay would be multiplied by 26, and so on.

Once an annualized gross figure is obtained, you multiply the standard deduction by the number of claimed dependents and subtract that from the annualized wage. This is the figure to which the computer applies its annualized tax tables. Although it may seem cumbersome, this system allows for much easier updates, and you have only one set of tax tables to worry about.

Software publishers offer a variety of update schemes for payroll tax information. Some will send you a floppy disk containing all tables in the original system, updated to reflect changed rates. Others will offer only printouts of changes and you must go into the tables manually and make the changes yourself. Still others offer updates free as part of the original selling price, while some charge a nominal or not-so-nominal fee.

When you're shopping for a payroll system, look for one that's likely to be supported fully and properly for a good length of time. At the least, make certain that your entire tax table file can be printed out for verification against government documents, and that you can manually edit entries on the tables if you must.

Transaction Processing

Time cards provide the primary source of transaction information into a payroll package. Of course, you may not use time cards per se, but if your employees have supervisors other than yourself, you probably receive a formal report of payroll particulars for each pay period. When you utilize a system with time cards and an entry screen for time card data, make certain two designs match each other to reduce the possibility of entry error.

Bonuses and commissions make up the other common form of payment information. Generally, they are entered into the system manually, for a particular pay period. If your business supports a stable bonus and/or commission structure (e.g., 15 percent of yearly salary at the end of the year), you may be able to enter this information as a default value in an employee's file, and also have it calculated automatically.

Transaction processing can be simple in a payroll system with mostly salaried workers. A day or two before the end of the pay period, you instruct the computer to prepare checks based on wages and other factors already present in the master file. Perhaps you enter an additional bonus for somebody, or note that a particular worker is on vacation this week, but that's all. A time card report or pay register is printed for review and edited before posting to the transaction file. You change the printer from its regular printout mode to its continuous check form mode, push a couple of keys, and—voila!—checks and a check register are produced automatically.

The payroll transaction file contains all information regarding income and deductions for the calendar year. This is the actual source file for paychecks and advances, and monthly, quarterly, and yearly reports (Forms 941 and W-2). One strong advantage of a computerized payroll system is that you instantly can produce period and year-to-date summaries out of this file. You can even produce W-2s and include them with the last paycheck of the year.

End-of-period processing includes printing the necessary forms and reports, and purging all but summary space from the transaction file. Reports may actually print onto the necessary federal/state payroll and tax forms, or they may be organized as worksheets, from which you manually complete the required forms. Either way, the storage and calculation efficiency of an automated system make end-of-period processing an easy job.

Payroll Outputs

Outputs from a payroll system are generated in a number of listings and reports, which include the following formats:

- Employee master list
- Employee detail listing

- Employee withholding report
- Beneficiary deduction report
- Quarterly earnings report
- W2s, 941s, and 940s
- Checks and paystubs

The employee master list of your employees should include at least the following information: rate and type of pay, hire date, number of deductions, marital status, and any special recurring deductions. The amount of detail on this list varies from program to program, so it's a good idea to ascertain that the package you are considering includes enough to meet your needs.

The employee detail listing itemizes the transactions for a particular employee, summarizes all monies earned for a particular period, and shows all deductions claimed. Usually, four sections can be found in this report: current pay figures, month-to-date figures, quarter-to-date figures, and year-to-date figures.

The employee withholding report itemizes and summarizes deductions taken from an employee's gross pay on a current, month-to-date, quarter-to-date, and year-to-date basis.

The beneficiary deduction report is basically a summary of the employee withholding report, grouped by deduction category rather than by individual employee. This report is a useful audit document as well as an aid in preparing tax forms for beneficiaries.

The quarterly earnings report is merely a summary of payroll registers for the quarter, grouped by employee. Almost all payroll systems also will produce government forms such as W-2s, 941s, and 940s. Some will even print 1099s for independent contractors.

All payroll packages reviewed in this book will print payroll checks and paystubs. Some also will print special or non-recurring checks for bonuses, abrupt terminations, one-time contract workers, spot incentives, and so on.

Other reporting features may be useful to your business. If you pay by mail, for example, a label-generating function that runs off the name and address of each employee is indispensable. Managers should enjoy the capacity to print reports listing employees with upcoming review dates or unused vacation time, and the ability to generate labor cost allocation reports for job-costing.

Converting to Automation

Chapter 3, "Charting Your Accounting Needs," describes the specific features you may expect to find in integrated accounting software, and it provides a Needs Assessment Checklist for you to match your requirements to what the market has to offer.

The bottom line is that you must determine your own needs and expectations before implementing a computerized accounting system. The types of questions you must answer include: How many different kinds of information do you intend to store in the system? What types of reports does your business require? Which accounting tasks consume the most time?

A common rule-of-thumb used by many accounting consultants to help clients determine what their needs are is as follows: If you can get a computer to perform from 60 to 80 percent of the work involved in an accounting task, then that task is an excellent candidate for automation. Some functions, however, may be best left to manual processing. A small company, for instance, may find that doing its payroll by hand is more cost-efficient, and that its accounts payable are not yet extensive enough to warrant automation. For the time being, this company might only want to use the general ledger and accounts receivable modules of an integrated accounting system.

Your first task, then, is to determine which area would most benefit from computerized books. Most businesses begin the conversion by automating their general ledger. This allows accounting personnel to acquaint themselves with computer operations, and reap the benefits of automated financial reporting, without the pressure of switching every accounting function at once. Then, when you add on other modules to create a fully integrated system, conversion should be a fairly smooth process.

Set up a conversion schedule that allows for acquisition and installation of your computer and software. Allocate time for entering such basic data as the company profile, customer lists, the chart of accounts, employee data, and inventory items. To determine the amount of time, effort, and expense you will require to accomplish these tasks, ask yourself the following questions:

- How many accounts do you have?
- What information must be recorded for each account?
- How organized are your current accounting records?
- At what point are you in your fiscal cycle?
- How fast will your accounting personnel be able to learn computer operations?
- Will data entry personnel have other responsibilities at the same time?
- Will you need to hire an outside consultant to help you convert?
- How closely does the software you are considering match your own accounting procedures?

Implementation of a computerized accounting system can take anywhere from a month to a year, depending on the size and complexity of your current system. No matter what the size of your business, you should run the computerized system and your former system side-by-side for at least one full quarterly cycle. Two or more quarters would be even better.

Running the two systems parallel allows your bookkeeping staff to become accustomed to new procedures. Inevitably, mistakes will occur during implementation of the new system, which makes concurrent maintenance of your manual system an imperative precaution. This obviously means that every accounting task will need to be performed twice, at least for a month or so, which will be a major factor to consider when scheduling time and resources.

The best time to convert is at the beginning of a fiscal cycle. This way, you can begin by entering only account balances into your new system, rather than duplicating all the transaction details that accompany day-to-day operations.

Finally, even though several people may be involved in data entry and transaction processing, you should assign the responsibility for daily operation of the system to just one person. A system manager should be responsible for maintaining security and audit controls, keeping records and data properly backed up, stocking supplies, maintaining equipment, and maintaining error, backup, and repair logs. Consolidating control over your system can make operating an automated accounting system smooth and free from serious error.

Chapter 3

Charting Your Accounting Needs

◆ With all of the accounting software products currently on the market, the selection of an appropriate package to meet your business needs presents a formidable challenge. Which program features are absolutely essential? Which are merely window dressing you can do without?

Your decision can be difficult even if you are familiar with other types of software, such as spreadsheets or database management systems. Therefore, the first step in selecting the best software program to take care of your accounting needs is to define exactly what those needs are.

This chapter examines some of the specific features and program aspects you should consider in choosing one or more of the five major accounting applications discussed in this book. It provides you with a Needs Assessment Checklist that is divided into two parts: a General Checklist and a Product Comparison Checklist.

The General Checklist asks such basic questions as: Why do you want an accounting software system? What are your intended applications? Who will actually operate the program? Additional questions concern your microcomputer system, its memory, and disk capacities. If you're in the process of buying a computer system, you'll be able to consider your software requirements as a major factor in making any hardware buying decision.

Next, you'll create a tentative list of products, based on the software programs presented in Part II of this book, which would appear to meet your accounting needs. Then, you'll use the Product Comparison Checklist to determine which accounting system is best for your business needs.

The Product Comparison Checklist is organized into sections that correspond to the product comparison charts found in Chapter 6. After exploring basic system requirements, documentation and support provisions, error handling, default settings, and security questions, this Checklist lets you examine the five accounting modules in detail. In this part of the Checklist, you'll compare three programs at once, feature by feature, in order to see at a glance which program offers you the best package.

Although this Needs Assessment Checklist can't itemize every possible accounting feature you might be interested in, it will walk you through the most important features and help you make an informed choice. Completing the Checklist also provides you with an easy means of creating your own evaluation tool.

GENERAL CHECKLIST

APPLICATIONS

1. Basic accounting functions you want to computerize:
   General Ledger _____
   Accounts Receivable _____
   Accounts Payable _____
   Inventory Control _____
   Payroll _____

   Additional accounting functions you want to computerize:
   Order Entry _____
   Fixed Asset Accounting _____
   Job Cost Tracking _____
   Budgeting _____
   Other specialized functions _____

2. System Users
   Number of users _____
   Level of user experience: (Use percentage)
   Beginner _____ Advanced _____
   Intermediate _____ Expert _____
   Number of users who will require training _____
   Training by: In-house user _____ Outside consultant _____

HARDWARE

3. Microcomputer _____

4. Operating system(s) _____

5. Total system memory (RAM) _____ K

6. Disk storage: Number of floppy disk drives _____
   Capacity of each floppy disk drive _____ K
   Total floppy capacity _____ K
   Capacity of hard disk _____ K
   Total system capacity _____ K

7. Printer _____

BUDGET AND PROGRAM SELECTION

8. Budget

	Software	**Hardware**
Initial purchase	$ _____	$ _____
Additional programs	$ _____	$ _____
Training aids/consultants	$ _____	$ _____
Total budget	$ _____	$ _____

9. List all integrated accounting programs in this book that meet your basic requirements, and are compatible with your computer and operating system(s).

1. _____   5. _____
2. _____   6. _____
3. _____   7. _____
4. _____   8. _____

10. From the previous list, select three programs that you want to compare in depth and use the numbers you assign them throughout the remainder of this worksheet.

Product Name	Publisher	Price
1. _____	_____	$ _____
2. _____	_____	$ _____
3. _____	_____	$ _____

PRODUCT COMPARISON CHECKLIST

BASIC INFORMATION

11. General considerations:

	1.	2.	3.
Operating system	1. _____	2. _____	3. _____
Minimum memory (RAM) required	1. _____	2. _____	3. _____
Hard disk required	1. ☐	2. ☐	3. ☐
Supports multiple users	1. ☐	2. ☐	3. ☐
Demo disk available	1. ☐	2. ☐	3. ☐
Phone support offered	1. ☐	2. ☐	3. ☐

Support terms
1. _____
2. _____
3. _____

DOCUMENTATION

12. Manual:

	1.	2.	3.
Index	1. ☐	2. ☐	3. ☐
Tutorial	1. ☐	2. ☐	3. ☐
Glossary of error messages	1. ☐	2. ☐	3. ☐
Glossary of terms	1. ☐	2. ☐	3. ☐

13. Other aids:

	1.	2.	3.
Tutorial on disk	1. ☐	2. ☐	3. ☐
Quick reference card	1. ☐	2. ☐	3. ☐

14. Online help:

	1.	2.	3.
Accessible at anytime	1. ☐	2. ☐	3. ☐
Context sensitive	1. ☐	2. ☐	3. ☐

GLOBAL FEATURES

15.

	1.	2.	3.
Maximum dollar amount allowed in transaction	1. _____	2. _____	3. _____
Decimal points automatic or manual	1. _____	2. _____	3. _____
Automatic format on date field	1. ☐	2. ☐	3. ☐
13-month accounting	1. ☐	2. ☐	3. ☐

16. Security: Password protection 1. ☐ 2. ☐ 3. ☐
            Multilevel security   1. ☐ 2. ☐ 3. ☐

17. Error handling: Automatic file backup   1. ☐ 2. ☐ 3. ☐
                    Indicates full disk   1. ☐ 2. ☐ 3. ☐
                    Full disk recovery procedure   1. ☐ 2. ☐ 3. ☐
                    Account numbers verified at time of entry 1. ☐ 2. ☐ 3. ☐
                    Error messages require acknowledgment or
                        other action   1. ☐ 2. ☐ 3. ☐

General Ledger Features

1. Maximum no. of accounts in your
       chart of accounts   1. _____ 2. _____ 3. _____
   Maximum no. of departments   1. _____ 2. _____ 3. _____
   Maximum no. of transactions per month 1. _____ 2. _____ 3. _____
   Maximum no. of journals   1. _____ 2. _____ 3. _____
   Recurring entries   1. ☐ 2. ☐ 3. ☐

2. Listings and reports: Chart of accounts listing   1. ☐ 2. ☐ 3. ☐
                         Trial balance worksheet   1. ☐ 2. ☐ 3. ☐
                         Budget listing   1. ☐ 2. ☐ 3. ☐
                         General ledger listing   1. ☐ 2. ☐ 3. ☐
                         Journal listing   1. ☐ 2. ☐ 3. ☐
                         General ledger closing report 1. ☐ 2. ☐ 3. ☐
                         Capital statement   1. ☐ 2. ☐ 3. ☐
                         Change in financial position 1. ☐ 2. ☐ 3. ☐
                         Balance sheet   1. ☐ 2. ☐ 3. ☐
                         Comparative balance sheet   1. ☐ 2. ☐ 3. ☐
                         Income statement   1. ☐ 2. ☐ 3. ☐
                         Comparative income statement 1. ☐ 2. ☐ 3. ☐
                         Depreciation and amortization
                             schedules   1. ☐ 2. ☐ 3. ☐
                         Comparative and current budget
                             reports   1. ☐ 2. ☐ 3. ☐
                         Budget variance reports   1. ☐ 2. ☐ 3. ☐

3. Reports can be: Year-to-date   1. ☐ 2. ☐ 3. ☐
                   Quarter-to-date   1. ☐ 2. ☐ 3. ☐
                   Other period-to-date 1. ☐ 2. ☐ 3. ☐

4. Built-in custom report generator   1. ☐ 2. ☐ 3. ☐

Accounts Receivable Features

1. Maximum no. of customers   1. _____ 2. _____ 3. _____
   Maximum no. of transactions per month 1. _____ 2. _____ 3. _____
   Maximum no. of departments   1. _____ 2. _____ 3. _____
   Open item accounts   1. ☐ 2. ☐ 3. ☐
   Balance forward accounts   1. ☐ 2. ☐ 3. ☐

	1.	2.	3.
Contract receivable accounts	☐	☐	☐
Recurring charges	☐	☐	☐
Optional order entry system	☐	☐	☐

2. Customer information:

	1.	2.	3.
Credit limit	☐	☐	☐
Terms net days	☐	☐	☐
Discounts by percentage	☐	☐	☐
Discounts by dollar amounts	☐	☐	☐
Salesperson code	☐	☐	☐

3. Processing information:

	1.	2.	3.
Credit memos	☐	☐	☐
Debit memos	☐	☐	☐
Automatically posts finance charges	☐	☐	☐
Automatic payment against oldest invoice first	☐	☐	☐

4. Query system:

	1.	2.	3.
Customer status by account number	☐	☐	☐
Customer status by invoice number	☐	☐	☐

5. Listings and reports:

	1.	2.	3.
Alphabetical listing of customers	☐	☐	☐
G/L consolidation and listing	☐	☐	☐
Statements	☐	☐	☐
Sales summary report	☐	☐	☐
Commission reports by salesperson	☐	☐	☐
Detail aged trial balance	☐	☐	☐
Custom formats	☐	☐	☐
Letters and labels	☐	☐	☐

Accounts Payable Features

1.

	1.	2.	3.
Maximum no. of vendors	_____	_____	_____
Maximum no. of transactions per month	_____	_____	_____
Maximum no. of departments	_____	_____	_____
Open item accounts	☐	☐	☐
Balance forward accounts	☐	☐	☐
Contract payable accounts	☐	☐	☐

2. Vendor information:

	1.	2.	3.
Terms net days	☐	☐	☐
Due date (day of month)	☐	☐	☐
Discounts by percentage	☐	☐	☐
Prompt payment discount	☐	☐	☐
Contact person	☐	☐	☐

3. Payment control entry:

	1.	2.	3.
Pay all invoices through (date)	☐	☐	☐
Manual check entry	☐	☐	☐
Specify payment date and starting check number	☐	☐	☐
Automatic payment against oldest invoice first	☐	☐	☐

4. Query system:

	1.	2.	3.
Vendor status by account number	☐	☐	☐
Vendor status by invoice number	☐	☐	☐

5. Listings and reports: Alphabetical listing of vendors   1. ☐   2. ☐   3. ☐

	1.	2.	3.
5. Listings and reports: Alphabetical listing of vendors	☐	☐	☐
Detail aged trial balance	☐	☐	☐
Checks and advice printing	☐	☐	☐
Posting journals	☐	☐	☐
Pre-check register	☐	☐	☐
Check register	☐	☐	☐
Cash requirements report	☐	☐	☐
Tax forms (1099)	☐	☐	☐
G/L consolidation and listing	☐	☐	☐
User-defined aging periods	☐	☐	☐
Letters/labels to vendors	☐	☐	☐

Inventory Control Features

	1.	2.	3.
1. Maximum no. of items	_____	_____	_____
Maximum no. of characters in item number	_____	_____	_____
Maximum no. of categories	_____	_____	_____
Purchase order and sales order systems	☐	☐	☐
Point-of-sale interface	☐	☐	☐
2. Item details: Maximum no. of characters in item description	_____	_____	_____
Quantity on hand	☐	☐	☐
Unit of measure	☐	☐	☐
Unit cost	☐	☐	☐
Unit price	☐	☐	☐
Quantity discount	☐	☐	☐
Period-to-date units sold	☐	☐	☐
Quantity on back order	☐	☐	☐
Quantity on purchase order	☐	☐	☐
Last source of supply	☐	☐	☐
Last cost	☐	☐	☐
Inventory location	☐	☐	☐
3. Processing: Physical inventory adjustments	☐	☐	☐
Track quantity committed to sales order	☐	☐	☐
Track quantity on purchase order	☐	☐	☐
Costing method	☐	☐	☐
4. Listings and reports: Price list	☐	☐	☐
Item status list	☐	☐	☐
Slow-moving items report	☐	☐	☐
Stock transfer listing	☐	☐	☐
Reorder report	☐	☐	☐
Under/over stock level reports	☐	☐	☐
G/L consolidation and summary report	☐	☐	☐
Physical inventory adjustments worksheet	☐	☐	☐
Bin and shelf labeling	☐	☐	☐
Item listing sorted by dollar volume	☐	☐	☐

Payroll Features

1. Maximum no. of employees   1._____   2._____   3._____

	1.	2.	3.
Cost accounting	☐	☐	☐
Multilevel overtime structure	☐	☐	☐
Special tax deductions	☐	☐	☐
Union withholdings	☐	☐	☐
Bonus	☐	☐	☐
Commissions	☐	☐	☐
Manual checks ability	☐	☐	☐
Mixed pay periods processing	☐	☐	☐
Mixed wage type processing	☐	☐	☐
Shift differentials hourly or by percentage	☐	☐	☐
Time card entry and verification	☐	☐	☐
User entry of federal and state tax tables	☐	☐	☐

2. Listings and reports:

	1.	2.	3.
Summary statistics	☐	☐	☐
Pay register	☐	☐	☐
941 and 940 forms	☐	☐	☐
W-2 forms	☐	☐	☐
Deductions register	☐	☐	☐
Vacation/sick time report	☐	☐	☐
FUTA report	☐	☐	☐
Tax table listings	☐	☐	☐
G/L consolidation and summary report	☐	☐	☐
Checks and pay stubs format adjustable	☐	☐	☐

Completing the Checklist

The remainder of this chapter discusses each numbered item on the entire Checklist and explains how to use this worksheet as a tool for making logical decisions about your accounting software needs. For additional explanations of unfamiliar terms or features, consult the Glossary or the Index in Part III of this book.

As previously explained, the General Checklist concerns essential questions about applications, hardware, and budget and program selection. The Product Comparison Checklist corresponds to the software comparison tables in Chapter 6. These questions involve basic information, product documentation and support, and include separate lists of program features and functions for each of the basic five accounting modules: general ledger, accounts receivable, accounts payable, inventory control, and payroll.

General Checklist

1. Determine the accounting functions that you would like to computerize in your company. Rank them in order from the most important function you want to implement to the least important. Under "additional accounting functions," note other activities you would like the computer to perform within the accounting system, such as order entry, budgeting, or fixed asset accounting.

2. For many companies, the major expense of converting to computerized accounting isn't the cost of the hardware and software, but the amount of time it takes to get the system online and fully operational. Therefore, any training aids and design features that encourage a smooth learning process for your computer operators have a true money value. If you do not have trained in-house personnel, there are many outside consulting firms who can do the initial training for you. This expense, however, can be a significant part of your budget.

Some dealers will offer hands-on training of the products they sell, in the form of workshops or seminars. Perhaps you can negotiate training for your users as part of the selling price. If you hire a consultant to come in and oversee the conversion process, make sure training provisions are spelled out. Some consultants specialize in training new users; you may decide this is a wise investment. Some software systems come with extensive training disks or online tutorials, which are training aids that teach you how to use a program during actual operation.

3-6. You'll need a computer, monitor, keyboard, and printer to computerize your accounting system. Include a 10-key numeric pad on the keyboard. This makes entering transactions easier and more accurate. The computer must have memory adequate to meet the software requirements. Most accounting software will require a hard disk, which is much faster and infinitely more reliable than floppy disk systems. For an application as crucial as accounting, the investment in a hard disk system is probably well worth the initial cost to your business.

7. A wide variety of printers exists on the market. Most accounting software generates a considerable amount of paper. If report and check generation are the main activity of your printer, and you won't need it for correspondence or other word processing functions, then choose a printer that offers high speed (120 to 300 characters per second).

8. A complete computer system with hard disk, high speed printer, and integrated accounting software easily can cost from $6,000 to $11,000 up front. But you should plan for the future growth of the system as well. As your business grows, you may decide to expand the computer's functions. You may find that you need a telecommunications modem, other terminals or computers that use the same printer or hard disk, or an additional printer. Don't forget to factor in training costs. A relatively inexpensive software package that's indecipherable to end users won't save you money in the long run.

9. By now you should at least have a general impression of your needs for accounting software. Based upon what you read regarding the software products in this book, narrow down the total list to only those products that basically meet your needs. See the Contents pages for the names of all products reviewed in this book.

10. From your preceding list, select three programs to compare simultaneously. Product publishers and prices are easily found in Chapter 6,

Table 6-1. You will use the numbers (1, 2, 3) you assign these products throughout the remainder of this Checklist, which is designed to help you compare three programs at once.

Product Comparison Checklist

Software is the most important piece of equipment in your accounting system. Most accounting software can't be modified to meet individual requirements. Therefore, it is imperative to choose software you can live with. If a piece of software doesn't perform a particular function that's crucial to your business, determine whether you can live without computerizing that function. If you can't, then choose another package.

Accounting software is designed to perform the basic functions required by most companies. As a software buyer, you must identify the unique aspects of your accounting system before looking for software. Obtain references from companies using a software package you're considering. Call on these companies if possible, and ask how well the system is working, how difficult it was to install, if support was needed, and if they recommend the package.

11. The operating system contains program instructions to allow communication between the operator and the application program. Make certain the program you want to purchase is available in a version that is compatible with your microcomputer's operating system.

System memory and type of storage form another major hardware consideration. The hardware system you use must have at least the minimum RAM required by the software program. A hard disk system will give you the greatest amount of storage space. If you elect to get a hard disk system, the program you select should be hard disk compatible.

Some accounting software comes in two versions: one for a single user, and one for multiple users. The latter is designed to be accessed through more than one microcomputer in a network configuration. If you plan to have more than one station online at a time, make certain your software is compatible with your desired arrangement.

A demo disk is a quick way to acquaint yourself with the way an accounting program functions. They usually show menus and input screens, and demonstrate some aspect of the system's transaction processing. Demo disks often are available for free or at a low cost from dealers or software publishers.

Most vendors provide some type of technical assistance for their products. Some companies provide it free for the first 30 to 90 days after purchase. Several others offer a toll-free hotline where you can talk with technicians trained in trouble-shooting their products. For some phone support arrangements, you pay a fee-per-minute or a fee-per-call. Still other companies have limited hours when technical support is available, or they are in a different time zone and their hours of availability do not neatly coincide with your hours of need. As a general rule, good accessible product support from a software house will cost you several hundred dollars a year.

Keep in mind that technical support is most important during the learning phase of your conversion from a manual to an automated accounting system. Most technical support departments will tell you that the same 10 or 12 problems habitually occur. Once your users have met and mastered this set of problems, you probably won't need to worry much about the quality of support available.

12. Documentation is often hard to evaluate. Appearances can be deceiving; don't be swayed merely by fancy packaging and high-quality paper. A three-ring binder is the most practical type of binding. It allows you to update the documentation, and the manual lays flat for easy use.

Some factors to look for in the manual of a quality package are: information on software installation and hardware configuration, a comprehensive index, a glossary or appendix specifically listing error messages and recommended action, a glossary of terms, step-by-step tutorials that explain a processing cycle, and a readable manual.

13. A tutorial on disk can give you a hands-on feel for program operations by letting you learn common commands in mock-up routines— without risking your own data. A quick reference card is useful when initially learning the program or performing once-a-month operations.

14. Online help means that the program provides information on the screen. Help that is accessible at any time, from any part of the program, usually is available through a special function key (e.g., F1), question mark or letter key. If user-assistance is context-sensitive, the help you request will be related directly to the activity currently in progress.

15. The maximum dollar amount in a transaction is one of the first things to check when you examine an accounting software package. Obviously, a system with one place-holder less than your anticipated highest amount would be of little use.

A number of programs will accept a date entry only in one specific format; others will guess the date from any reasonable approximation. Formats for columns of digits can have similar default settings and irritations.

Some businesses prefer to divide their fiscal year into 13 ''months,'' each 28 days in length. This makes, among other things, comparisons of business activities from period to period more accurate. If your company prefers this arrangement, select an accounting system that can conform to your procedures, rather than adapting to one that does not.

16. If you have several different kinds of potential users for your system, it may be wise to select your software with multilevel password protection as a priority. If your office is smaller, with only one or two users whose duties overlap, it may be more feasible simply to control access to the equipment.

17. A backup disk provides a complete and portable copy of your valuable information. This copy of your important data can be stored in a remote location or fireproof safe to protect against disaster.

Backup procedures are simple to follow and require little time. An accounting system with good internal controls forces you to make backup copies of your data at certain times—usually before a posting or during a purge function when data is added or removed from a file and sorted. A regular, complete backup program is the best protection you can have against operator, hardware, and electrical mishaps.

The way your software identifies errors and the resources it offers you for correcting them can be an important consideration when buying a system. Some software documentation will include a glossary or appendix of error messages which lists error descriptions and suggestions for solving the problem. Some programs present messages on the screen identifying a problem that has occurred. If the system you are considering offers these error-handling features, look for clarity of explanation and the subsequent recommendation.

Error messages are built into accounting software to alert the user about improper entries and hardware or software malfunctions. These messages can be grouped into three basic categories: warnings, procedural errors, and system errors.

An *error warning* alerts the operator to minor errors, such as an invalid date entry, or an account number that doesn't exist in the master file. Often, the program will simply erase your entry and prompt you to try again. Sometimes a warning may be triggered by information that is accurate but unlikely—for instance, a transaction date that represents a different fiscal period than the current one.

A *procedural error* indicates an invalid sequence of operations. For example, you might attempt to clear information from the system before the necessary audit trails have been printed. The program knows that proper accounting practice requires a particular sequence, and it will not execute your instructions. Instead, most systems will display a message advising you of correct procedure.

The most serious errors are called *system errors,* which result in a halt of system operations until the problem is corrected. The source of the error may be a flaw in a memory chip or a disk, or it may be the result of a sudden power surge. In any case, system errors may result in loss of data, although some software suppliers provide programs that will recoup some, if not all, of your losses.

General Ledger Features

1. Count the current number of accounts in your chart of accounts, allowing for growth over the next two years. A safe estimate is usually two or two-and-a-half times the current number. Some accounts may be retired during this period and deleted at the end of the fiscal year, but you also will add new accounts.

Take a good look at how the chart of accounts is organized in your current manual system. How many fields of necessary information does each account hold now? What identifying scheme is already in use? Do you use three-digit codes with an ''A'' designating assets, an ''L'' for liabilities, and so on?

When you're evaluating software, compare your own method of handling accounts to the one used by the automated accounting product you are considering. Can you make a conversion with relative ease, or will you need to completely restructure the way your records are organized? For instance, if you're considering a G/L package that limits asset account categories to no more than three, and your current manual system utilizes a breakdown by five separate asset accounts, that package will cost you extra time and effort to utilize.

If the general ledger you select permits departmental accounting, make sure the maximum number of departments tracked will be sufficient both now and in the future. The same provision regarding future growth goes for the maximum number of transactions and journals.

2. These items involve the standard listings and reports required by most G/L operations. Check the ones you use to make your management decisions, and note those that are interesting, but not absolutely necessary. If flexible computerized analysis of accounting information is one of your principal reasons for automating, there's no need to settle for a package with limited reporting capabilities. Many modules will go beyond the standard array of listings and reports and include a useful selection of comparative financial statements.

Even though computerization eliminates a lot of the paperwork associated with accounting, you'll still need good organization for the printouts you generate. Classify your hardcopy into proper categories. Label all reports with the date and time of printout. Outdated reports should be filed temporarily in case you need them for reference, and you should file audit listings separately for easy access. If you need to reconstruct data that somehow has been lost from both a data disk and its backup, hardcopy may be able to save the day.

3-4. Year-to-date and quarter-to-date reports are standard in the majority of G/L packages. If a program will allow you to isolate other periods, however, you have that much more flexibility in analyzing your business activities.

G/L modules with built-in custom report generators almost always allow you to vary the period length of a report. They also offer you an unlimited number of formats and let you group financial information, by almost any criteria, on your hardcopy. Generally, packages that have custom report generators also will include a few fixed formats, although some require you to establish them all yourself. At the other extreme, a number of G/L modules that lack custom formatting offer such an abundance of fixed format reports, you'd be hard pressed to come up with more.

Accounts Receivable Features

1. To estimate the maximum number of accounts you will need in your customer file, count the current number of customers you've done business with over the past year. Omit any you've dealt with only once, or who only paid cash. Estimate the number of customers you expect to attract within the next two years, and add this to the previous figure to come up with your projected maximum.

The number of transactions per month includes payments and adjustments. Count as a separate transaction any account activity which would be listed on an individual line in a manual A/R ledger.

Nearly all A/R modules will give you the option of handling your customers as either balance forward or open item accounts. Typically, customers that order often or in large quantities want the increased detail afforded by the open item method. Make certain the A/R module you select will allow you to include enough detail on statements to satisfy your customers' needs. Remember, however, that open item accounts require a greater amount of disk space than their balance forward counterparts.

A recurring charges function automatically assigns a predetermined monthly charge to specified customer accounts. Contract receivables are a special type of recurring charge, determined by terms of a contract established between you and your customer. Both these periodic functions automatically debit customer accounts according to parameters set up at the beginning of a fiscal period.

In some cases, order entry capabilities reside in the A/R module. More often, you must enter customer orders and print out invoices through a separate order entry module that integrates with accounts receivable. Generally, this module also ties into inventory control, subtracting items according to the quantities listed on customer invoices.

If most of your invoices are handwritten, or if most of your sales are in cash, this capability is probably unnecessary. But if you take many phone or mail orders, or if you send numerous invoices by mail, make certain your integrated accounting system offers order entry as a function of your A/R package, within inventory control, or (more likely) as a separate, compatible module.

2. Use this section to evaluate the amount of customer detail you require, and the amount an A/R package's master file will hold. The detail in the customer file is used as a basis for generating reports, and for controlling the information that will be available when you use a query system. Some A/R packages offer an abundance of information fields—too much, in fact, for certain businesses. Ideally, a customer file with plenty of detail will let you bypass the data input fields you feel are unnecessary.

3. Check the functions you require when processing accounts receivable. If you are running your accounts on an open item basis, features such as "automatic payment against oldest invoice first" can be a real time saver. "Automatic posting of finance charges" may be only one of the special posting routines required by your company.

4. All systems generate printed reports reflecting account details. But if you must have immediate access to this information on your monitor, a flexible query system is crucial. Query systems generally retrieve information by account number; some systems will look up accounts based upon alphabetical information as well.

5. The listings and reports shown here are the most common outputs of an A/R module. Decide which reports are necessary for your business management first, then pick out the less essential ones.

Many listings and reports contain the same information organized in a different order. One company, for instance, may produce a set of weekly sales summary reports. Each of these reports shows the same basic data, but one report lists sales in invoice order and the other lists sales by salesperson. In some cases, businesses with more unique reporting requirements may need formats provided by only a few A/R products.

Accounts Payable Features

1. The maximum number of vendors in your master file can be gauged by adding your current number to that which you may expect to add within the next two years. Don't bother to count vendors with whom you've done businesses only once or twice.

Remember that the number of transactions per month includes both payments and adjustments. As in accounts receivable, count as a separate transaction any account activity that would be listed on an individual line in a manual payables ledger.

An A/P module, like its A/R counterpart, usually handles accounts by either the open item or balance forward method. Flexible packages also will let you change methods as needed.

Contract payable accounts are the flip side of contract receivables. If you frequently deal with vendors on a contractual basis, make certain your A/P package has this feature.

2. Terms and discounts can be difficult to keep track of, especially if you deal with a large number of vendors. An A/P package should hold enough information to accommodate relevant variations from vendor to vendor. With certain vendors, staying on top of your payables can get you prompt payment discounts on a regular basis.

If your A/P vendor file has a field for vendor contact, the information therein can be particularly helpful when using a query system. If an invoice is under dispute, for example, an effective query system will not only generate an onscreen display of a given account balance, but also list whom you should contact to help settle the matter.

3. The features found in the payment control entry of an A/P package dictate how smoothly your payables processing will function. It's important to choose an A/P module that handles payment of invoices on the schedule you choose. You may be interested in the module's ability to take discounts, to make partial payments, to avoid payment entirely on some accounts, and to recognize when manual checks have been issued.

4. The query system is of utmost importance if you require fast access to your accounts payable information. For example, if a vendor ships you a C.O.D. item you weren't expecting, you might want to execute a query on all recent transaction details before issuing a check. As in accounts receivable, a good query system should be able to retrieve this information by account number or name.

5. Payables listings and reporting requirements vary from business to business. A company that routinely offers its services through private contractors, for example, may wish to list its subcontracted work on a separate report. This helps determine whether in-house personnel could accomplish a job on a more cost-effective basis.

In general, this company would look for special report formats that track costs associated with private contractors. The ability to generate tax forms (i.e., 1099s) also would be a necessity.

Inventory Control Features

1. The number of items in your inventory undoubtedly will fluctuate to a greater extent than the number of vendor or customer accounts. Therefore, allow more leeway in your estimate of a maximum number than you would in A/R or A/P.

The number of characters in your item number will be determined in part by the type of business you operate. Most inventory control systems are designed to perform one major type of inventory function. If you are a retail operation, you may require a point-of-sale system to record inventory transactions. If you value inventory on an item-by-item basis, you may need specific item identification, such as tracking serial numbers. If you are a wholesaler or a retailer, you probably need a purchasing order and sales order system for entering and recording transactions.

Equally important is the selection of an inventory system that properly identifies items by category, class, group, and product line. Generally, these breakdowns are identified by segments within the item number itself.

2-3. Inventory item details include information kept on file and maintained by the system. This is also the basic information for generating reports and processing inventory transactions. Look for a system that supports the type of costing you presently use, and how you keep track of committed orders and quantities on order.

4. A wide variety of reports is available from a computerized inventory control package. In most manual systems, very few of the report possibilities are exploited, due to the amount of time and effort it takes to compile the appropriate information. An automated system can give you the kind of timely feedback you need to streamline your inventory and tighten control over your stocking procedures.

When you evaluate an inventory control package, review the sample reports provided with the program documentation. Make certain the package provides the reports most valuable to you, and in the format best suited to your inventory procedures.

Payroll Features

1. The way in which a payroll system operates varies little from package to package. This is because payroll methods are dictated by federal, state, and local law. Sometimes the complex, shifting tax requirements involved in payroll processing can be quite confusing.

Payroll systems maintain a file of tax tables that affect nearly all aspects of payroll calculation. Some software publishers offer free tax table updates for a specified period of time as part of a package's selling price. Others provide this service for a fee. In some instances, you may have to manually enter all tax changes.

You must also take into account the variety of pay periods, wage types, overtime classifications, and special withholdings and deductions required by your employees. These parameters can be nearly as complicated as those defined by tax laws. The ease with which a payroll module handles such variations is a measure of its sophistication.

2. Listings and reports produced by any payroll system are very valuable for completing federal, state, and local forms. Some systems actually print on these forms, while others prepare a worksheet containing most of the necessary information.

Make certain the paystubs you print out contain all the information your employees require. In addition, if your format is adjustable, then there's no need to worry about obtaining check and paystub forms that follow a fixed format.

Part II

Integrated Accounting Software

Chapter 4

Reviewing the Benchmark Product

❖ The EasyBusiness Systems, from Sorcim/IUS, is arguably the "Cadillac" of integrated accounting software packages. The total series of seven products blends sound accounting practices, programming saavy, and smooth user interface into a full-service accounting and financial reporting system that continues to grow in sales popularity.

The original EasyBusiness Systems was developed several years ago by the Basic Software Group of Vancouver, Canada. In 1980, it began American distribution as part of Northstar Computer's proprietary operating system. Information Unlimited Software (IUS) began its involvement with EasyBusiness Systems the following year by acquiring distribution rights for the MS-DOS version of the program. This meant that EasyBusiness Systems could be sold to the burgeoning IBM Personal Computer and PC-compatible market.

Within a few years, however, the distribution rights to EasyBusiness Systems changed hands once again. In late 1983, IUS was acquired by Computer Associates International, which in turn merged IUS with another of its acquisitions, the Sorcim Corporation, to create Sorcim/IUS. The Sorcim Corporation was responsible for SuperCalc, an extremely popular and highly successful spreadsheet software series. Finally, in 1984, Sorcim/IUS introduced its combined line of software products, including the EasyBusiness Systems Plus Series, which features both accounting and productivity software.

Quite a product history, but not unusual in the volatile microcomputer software industry. Despite the change of hands and several concomitant physical moves, product support for EasyBusiness Systems has remained steady and reliable. Since these products also have kept pace with the newest software technologies, including windowing and data-transfer capabilities, it's no surprise that the EasyBusiness Systems is still a market favorite.

Although each of the accounting modules in the latest version (Version 4.0) of this system can operate in a stand-alone capacity, this chapter will focus on the modules as an integrated whole. A close examination of the many features and functions of this system will provide you with a "benchmark," or standard measure of comparison, in evaluating the other accounting software programs reviewed in this book.

EasyBusiness Systems

COMPANY:	Sorcim/IUS Micro Software
REQUIREMENTS:	PC-DOS or MS-DOS; 128K; two disk drives or hard disk; 132-column printer.
COMPATIBILITY:	Order Entry; EasyPlus; EasyFiler; EasyWriter II System; EasyPlanner; SuperProject; SuperCalc.
PRICE:	General Ledger & Financial Reporter ($595); Accounts Receivable ($595); Accounts Payable ($595); Inventory Control & Analysis ($595); Payroll ($745). Total price: $3,220.

The EasyBusiness Systems package includes five basic accounting modules: General Ledger and Financial Reporter, Accounts Receivable, Accounts Payable, Inventory Control and Analysis, and Payroll. A sixth module, Order Entry, integrates with Accounts Receivable and Inventory Control to provide automatic invoicing and an extensive onscreen query utility. (Time, Billing, and Client Receivables programs also have been announced, but were not available when this review was conducted.)

An additional software program called EasyPlus provides a "windowing system" (more on this later) that allows you to integrate the Plus Series modules—which include the six EasyBusiness Systems accounting programs and three productivity programs: EasyFiler (an information management system), EasyWriter II System (a word processing program), and EasyPlanner (a spreadsheet program). EasyPlus supports concurrent processing of up to 10 windows, each representing a separate Plus Series application.

You'll need a minimum of 256K RAM to run EasyPlus and one accounting module. In order to take full advantage of the program's integrated capabilities, however, more memory is required. With 512K, for example, you can run EasyPlus and the basic five accounting modules.

EasyPlus has an extensive custom format feature. You can manipulate placement and size relationships of the onscreen windows to suit your own particular needs. If you have five or six windows going at once, however, they must be designed carefully (color coded, if possible) to avoid a confusing, cluttered screen.

The use of windows is ideal for integrated accounting software. One window can handle order entry while another can take care of customer maintenance or accounts receivable. If a customer is not on file for the order being entered, you can jump to the A/R window, enter the new customer, and continue placing the order. Setting field lengths and column alignments to match precisely between modules allows you to transfer data, character-by-character, from one module to another. A further advantage in installing the EasyPlus windowing system and application manager first is that you only have to configure your printer once, rather than for each module you install.

Each module in the EasyBusiness Systems package has its own manual. The documentation is bound in a standard, three-ring binder and printed on high-quality bond. A second color sets off screen display illustrations, and special sections are delineated clearly and colorfully.

The sample input forms included in each binder reveal a considerate attitude toward the end user. These forms can be copied and used when you must collect data by hand, and are particularly useful if someone other than the computer operator prepares the information to be entered into the system.

The manuals also provide useful appendices, including one that explains how to accommodate a wide selection of popular printers. In addition, glossaries, indices, and other information unique to each module are included in every manual.

Each module in the EasyBusiness Systems package offers well-designed online tutorials. A sample database accompanies every module, offering representations of a wide variety of accounting situations. You can alter and process the sample database until you understand how the programs operate.

A context-sensitive online help system allows instant access to additional information about the process you are performing. As with any context-sensitive help utility, you only receive information pertinent to the task at hand. Supported by the EasyPlus windowing system, online help may be obtained at any time from within any module by simply pressing the F3 function key on your keyboard. Whenever you press F3, a window opens on the screen to reveal an explanation of the operation in progress.

The help messages themselves are well written, offering clear and concise explanations of each program aspect. If the information you are requesting isn't in the current help window, you can press F3 to find the help screen you need. While using EasyPlus, however, a help window will require an extra 20-30K of RAM.

All modules within the system are completely menu driven. A master menu summarizes the major tasks of the accounting module in use. After you make a selection from the master menu, a submenu appears and displays different functions within that task. Selection from the submenu refers you to a "video form," a term used throughout the documentation to denote onscreen blank fields such as the one used for the company profile.

Once you learn the menu system for one of the modules, the others are easy. All menu selections are simple, one-key commands. The Enter (or Return) key is used always as a "Yes" or "Continue" command, while the Escape key acts as a "No" or "Ignore" command. This uniformity cuts down on the time spent learning the system and helps eliminate confusion when switching from module to module.

Another major factor to consider in reviewing the advantages of EasyBusiness Systems is the fact that its users receive first-class support from Sorcim/IUS. Since most problems arise within the initial startup phase, a phone support program is provided free for six months. Long-term support is on a subscription basis; for an annual fee, you are privy to the toll-free number for the support center, and discounts on new versions and updates.

Using the Big Five Modules

This section outlines many of the important features and functions you'll find in each of the five basic accounting modules which comprise the EasyBusiness Systems. Comments on important program considerations and day-to-day operations are included. Illustrations of a few typical reports, listings, and display screens have been included to provide you with a general picture of what it is like to operate the various programs.

General Ledger & Financial Reporter

The EasyBusiness Systems' General Ledger and Financial Reporter module automatically performs all the tedious recordkeeping functions of a manual system. It allows you to create G/L accounts and to maintain transactions from a variety of sources. In addition, the wide assortment of listings and financial reports generated by this module is exceptional.

You can establish up to 10 source journals for such categories as cash disbursements and cash receipts. When you enter a particular transaction in the general ledger, an appropriate source code is specified. Later, you can use this code to sort your data and produce a journal of, say, all cash receipts for the period.

If you want to generate comparative financial statements, historical information can be entered for each account for up to 12 accounting periods. The budget calculator feature makes provisions for 12 separate budget amounts within a single report.

The chart of accounts provides for a 12-character alphanumeric account number, the last six places of which generally indicate cost centers. The financial reporting system does not depend upon the account number order. Therefore, when you set up the chart of accounts, similar accounts need not be grouped together for reporting purposes.

The G/L application program accepts transactions in batch form and checks them for existing account numbers, correct fiscal period, and balanced entry prior to posting. To eliminate rekeying any transactions that remain unchanged from period to period, you can set up recurring entries by archiving a batch of transactions and instructing the program to retrieve the batch at a later date.

As shown in Figure 4-1, the General Ledger and Financial Reporter module provides a special feature, called the "Quick Entry" form, for entering transactions that need distribution to different accounts. This offers you the convenience of entering transaction details just once. The program then asks you for the amount of the transaction, and the account to which you want the transaction distributed. This provides a handy "sub-batch" capacity when, for example, you want to deposit a check in one account and distribute the funds to cover several transactions in other accounts.

```
THE UNIVERSAL CORPORATION                          Date: Feb 09 85
Quick Entry and Distribution


     Batch Number [3  ] has          Transactions.
     ------------------------------------------------------------
         Period        [  ]
         Source        [ ]
         Date          [  /  /  ]
         Reference     [       ]
         Description   [                              ]

         Account       [       ] Dept.[      ]
         Amount           Dr.[              ] Cr.[              ]




     Press ESCAPE to exit.
```

FIGURE 4-1 EasyBusiness Systems Quick Entry Form

Transactions also can be obtained from the A/R, A/P, Inventory Control and Analysis, and Payroll modules, simply by indicating from which module you wish to extract the information. The transfer of information from the other modules is independent of all other accounting functions, and can be handled through the windowing system in several ways. Distribution detail is maintained by the individual module, and each module consolidates the information internally before transferring it to the general ledger.

A batch of transactions remains open for editing up until the time it's posted to the general ledger. Before actual distribution to G/L accounts, the program demands that a trial balance worksheet, as seen in Figure 4-2, be sent to the printer for proofing. Once this audit trail listing has been printed, the program automatically will post all batches to the general ledger, including those transactions that were unavailable when the general ledger closed for the year—such as depreciation figures or discount amounts. Closing the ledger brings the balance sheet accounts forward to start the new fiscal year, and clears all income/expense accounts for the new year by entering profit/loss information to the retained earnings account.

The General Ledger and Financial Reporter has one of the most complete report writers available for microcomputer accounting. Creating a report requires that you issue a set of commands telling the report generator what information to take from the general ledger. You also must select such format specifications as rows, field lengths, and the number of columns.

While this takes more time initially than simply using default report configurations of the kind offered by other systems, the long-term benefits of reports tailored to your specific needs are substantial.

There are 38 categories and numerical relationships available to the reporting system for each G/L. These include: opening balance; current balance; current 12-month account totals; previous 12-month account totals; and 12 months of budget information for each account.

Reports can be categorized by individual departments, or they can encompass a range of departments. If you wish, all departments can be consolidated to produce a report containing every company in your system. You can ask the report generator to use account titles from the chart of accounts, or you can enter your own description. A report can contain up to nine columns, and multiple-page reports can be combined to provide a single report. A column in the report can contain any of the 38 categories and numerical relationships listed above, including period ranges from the current or previous year. A column can be expressed as the difference between two other columns in actual numbers, in percentages, or as a ratio to any numerical expression or category within the report.

The specification editor takes several hours to learn, but it's well worth the effort. The analytical flexibility obtainable with the specification editor, together with the budget calculator, comes close to equaling that of many powerful spreadsheet programs. Accounting firms that specialize in write-up work, or any business that requires diverse, specialized reports, will find many valuable features within the EasyBusiness Systems' General Ledger and Financial Reporter module.

Accounts Receivable

The EasyBusiness Systems' Accounts Receivable module supports both open item and balance forward accounts. In open item accounts, the system automatically applies the payment to the oldest invoices first. You can override this feature and apply a payment to any invoice or series of invoices you want. Open or unapplied credit also can be entered and adjusted to the invoices at a later date.

The system supports recurring charges, and will track on demand the average time it takes for a customer to pay his or her bills. You can override statements on an account-by-account basis, and set up the billing so interest is charged automatically to accounts with balances that exceed their credit terms. Using the EasyWriter II System, which includes a mail merge program, you easily can prepare mailing labels and custom letters for accounts owing your company money beyond a certain time period.

An onscreen query system, shown in Figure 4-3, provides instant information on any account, including invoice and payment detail, and account aging information. You also can review customer totals to reflect an aging distribution at the company level.

Invoices, adjustments, and payments are entered, edited, and posted through similar procedures. Each of these transaction categories has its own menu, input screen, and audit trail facility. After invoices are posted, for example, the audit trail can be printed in the invoice form. Or, it can be listed as a customer order, as an invoice journal in invoice order, or as both.

THE UNIVERSAL CORPORATION   Page: 1

August 31, 1984

Trial Balance Worksheet

Current fiscal period: 2

Acct Code	Dept Code	Account Name	Trial Balance Debit	Trial Balance Credit	Adjustments Debit	Adjustments Credit	Income Statement Debit	Income Statement Credit	Balance Sheet Debit	Balance Sheet Credit
100		Petty cash	0.00							
102		Cash on hand	0.00							
104		Bank – Operating	0.00							
105		Bank – Foreign Exchange	0.00							
106		Bank – payroll	0.00							
200		Accounts receivable – trade	0.00							
202		Accounts receivable–employees	0.00							
204		Accounts receivable – other	0.00							
210		Allowance for doubtful accts.	0.00							
250		Inventory	0.00							
300		Prepaid expenses	0.00							
350		Investments	0.00							
400		Land	0.00							
402		Buildings	0.00							
404		Leasehold improvements	0.00							
406		Furniture & fixtures	0.00							
408		Machinery & equipment	0.00							
422		Accum. depr.–buildings	0.00							

FIGURE 4-2 EasyBusiness Systems Trial Balance Worksheet

```
THE UNIVERSAL CORPORATION                    Date: May 03 85
Review Account Details

Customer Number [   200]  Chloride Systems

Last invoice on Mar 03 85   Amount:   13,840.42
Last payment on Mar 13 85   Amount:   13,563.61

Year to date sales:      13,840.42
Last year's sales:       13,688.88

Outstanding transactions: 2
     Balance outstanding:          0.00



Enter opening invoice number: [            ]
```

FIGURE 4-3 EasyBusiness Systems Query Screen

The A/R module also can import transactions from other, non-EasyBusiness Systems software. This is accomplished through the use of a file that must be prepared in a specific format, utilizing the system's operating system (PC/MS-DOS). Most spreadsheet programs that use a "print to file" function can be set up to export data to the A/R module, and so can database management programs that support popular data file formats. Once imported, these transactions are treated the same as manually entered ones.

Accounts Payable

The EasyBusiness Systems' Accounts Payable module performs the entire bill-paying sequence from entry of vendor invoices to automatic check printing. The onscreen query system found in this module provides instant details for any account, including invoices, payments, discounts taken, and account aging information.

As in the A/R module, similar procedures for entering various types of transactions are employed, and each transaction type has a different input screen and menu. This design consistency helps enhance learning speed and ease-of-use. Also like the A/R program, the A/P module allows you to import transactions from software outside the EasyBusiness Systems programs, again through a specially formatted DOS file.

Manual checks are entered as adjustments. The program prepares a pre-check register, shown in Figure 4-4, that reflects which invoices and

Date: Mar 01 85   THE UNIVERSAL CORPORATION   Page: 1

Pre-Check Register for Vendors [   ] to [zzzzzz] on Mar 01 85 until Mar 08 85   Taking Discounts

CODES: P - Max. payment controlled;   S - Special discount base.

Vendor Number	Vendor Name	Invoice Number	Discount/ Due Date	Gross	Discount	Net
540	Hart Batteries	75101	Mar 05 85	800.66	0.00	800.66
				800.66*	0.00*	800.66*
5000	Deca Management	JAN	Jan 17 85	1,250.00	0.00	1,250.00
				1,250.00*	0.00*	1,250.00*
5010	Designer's Corner	JAN	Jan 18 85	282.31	0.00	282.31
				282.31*	0.00*	282.31*
5030	Donald & Donald	JAN	Jan 17 85	500.00	0.00	500.00
				500.00*	0.00*	500.00*
8950	Vulcan & Sons	523	Feb 01 85	246.91	0.00	246.91
				246.91*	0.00*	246.91*
Totals of 5 check(s) to be issued				3,079.88	0.00	3,079.88

FIGURE 4-4 *EasyBusiness Systems Pre-Check Register*

discounts will be taken. After reviewing the pre-check register, you are provided with a special screen for entering payment control information. Partial payment can be made on an entire account, or on specific invoices. After the program prints the checks, it prints out an actual check register that includes check numbers to serve as the audit trail. You can write checks against a maximum of five bank accounts.

Inventory Control & Analysis

One of the most powerful features of the EasyBusiness Systems' Inventory Control and Analysis module is the custom-formatting feature for inventory item numbers. The item number is divided into four segments, each of which may be up to 16 characters long. This gives you more than enough flexibility to use your existing item numbers, while adding various characters as control indicators for sophisticated tracking of inventory movement.

A six-level pricing system offers automatic volume discounts and customer price-list tables. Inventory can be costed by one of three methods: LIFO, FIFO, or weighted moving average. The inventory package includes an option to retain sales units, sales dollars, and cost-of-sales for each item for the previous year, the current year-to-date, the current period, or the last four custom periods. This information is used subsequently to prepare a wide variety of analytical reports that help you to effectively control your inventory by graphically displaying various determining trends and sales patterns.

With this module, you can specify up to 999 departments. Cost-of-sales can be reported automatically to the general ledger by using these categories. Two warehouses can be supported, for example, and complete control for stock transfers is supplied. Over 50 other fields are available for maintaining and tracking information on each inventory item. By choosing the options you want for your own particular configuration, you can customize the package to maintain the information you find most valuable. The sales, cost-of-sales, and net inventory valuation changes are collected automatically for reporting to the general ledger.

Sorcim/IUS also offers an Order Entry module that integrates with A/R and Inventory Control and Analysis. The Order Entry module provides an onscreen query system to check current stock levels, to help determine pricing, to generate picking and packing slips, and to record the information necessary for reporting sales to the general ledger.

Back orders and standing orders also are maintained in memory and processed automatically, even if you forget. Credit limits can be checked and flagged if necessary, and the system can assign customers a tax status for automatic calculation.

Payroll

The EasyBusiness Systems' Payroll module is designed to perform all payroll functions for small- to medium-sized businesses. Payroll information is divided into six different categories, each of which contains a specific type of information necessary for the payroll processing cycle.

The company master records maintain the company profile, and also divide personnel into specific categories, such as direct labor, administrative, and sales personnel. G/L codes are used to collect and identify information that will be transferred to the general ledger during end-of-month processing.

The employee master record shown in Figure 4-5 stores the individual employee's personnel and wage information and cross-references it to tax tables. This information is used to calculate taxes, quarter-to-date, and year-to-date figures. Employee detail records contain employee deductions, employer contributions, and non-standard sources of income, such as commission. Each employee master record has associated detail records for all payroll transactions to include all deductions.

The tax tables provide guidelines used by the system to calculate payroll taxes. When tax rates change, these tables can be created and altered. The tax tables system will support employees for a work state, for a resident state, for city and county taxes, and for federal taxes. FICA and special withholding taxes are handled by a special set of tables.

Net pay is calculated for each employee for the pay period. Using salary or time-card information and the tax tables developed in the system, itemized deductions and withholdings are arrived at automatically, and the payroll register is presented for proofing. Paychecks then may be printed, along with detailed reports summarizing payroll activity for the period. You may print end-of-month, end-of-quarter, and end-of-year reports at the appropriate intervals to meet government requirements.

In order to keep your Payroll module updated with the latest tax guidelines, Sorcim/IUS provides a separate ''Tax Updater'' disk and a toll-free number as part of its support system. Occasionally, changes in the tax structure are so complicated that a modification of the program may be required. Sorcim/IUS will update your software accordingly if such complex changes become necessary. If you subscribe to the support program, all tax table updates are made at no charge. This is one of the most complete payroll support services available, and worth the price of the package itself if you have complicated payroll processing requirements.

Overall Performance

The comments in this section are based on a series of comprehensive tests by several accounting software users who evaluated each of the EasyBusiness Systems accounting modules featured in this chapter. These tests utilized the evaluation and review criteria found in Appendix A of Part III.

First, the overall performance of the EasyBusiness Systems is excellent. Data files are maintained by a complex method of indexing, and looking up data and verifying it is a fast and accurate procedure.

All of the system's menus are retained in memory, resulting in speedy access to any part of the system at anytime. The screen and menu formats are detailed and consistent, and the organization of the system is so logical, you can learn where to find the information you need in a remarkably short period of time.

The pre-formatted listings and reports generated by the system have been designed carefully, and the reports present the information in a clear,

```
Date: Apr 04 85   Universal Corporation                         Page:  1

                  March 31, 1985

                  Employee Master, Tax and *TD Listing

Employee Number:       1
Last:             Dole
First:            Roland              Initial: Z
Address:          52000 Independence Boulevard
                  Madison
                  Wisconsin
Zip Code:         53714
S.S. Number:      391477822           Status: A
Dept. Number:        100              Name: Research & Development
Employment Date:  Jan 01 85
Termination Date: ??? 00 00
Pay Type:         S                   Frequency: W
Shift Number:     1
Normal Hours:        40.0             Hourly Rate:          0.00
Salary:                 1,000.00

Salary Distribution:
G/L Account:                          Rate:    .0
G/L Account:                          Rate:    .0
G/L Account:                          Rate:    .0

Deduct Federal?   Y                   Federal Status:  M
Exemptions:       0                   Extra:           0.00
Work State I.D.:  WI                  State Status:    M
Exemptions        0                   Extra:           0.00
Res. State I.D.:  0                   State Status:
Exemptions:       0                   Extra:           0.00
County I.D.:      0                   County Status:
Exemptions:       0                   Extra:           0.00
City I.D.:        0                   City Status:
Exemptions:       0                   Extra:           0.00

Employee's Taxes Withheld to Date.
                  MTD            QTD            YTD
Federal:          1,061.54       3,203.13       3,203.13
FICA:               271.35         817.40         817.40
Work State:         318.31         959.68         959.68
Res. State:           0.00           0.00           0.00
County:               0.00           0.00           0.00
City:                 0.00           0.00           0.00

Employee's Wages to Date.
                  MTD            QTD            YTD
Regular:          2,500.00       10,000.01      10,000.01
Overtime:             0.00            0.00           0.00
Shift Diff:           0.00            0.00           0.00
Gross:            4,050.00       12,199.99      12,199.99
Federal:          4,050.00       12,199.99      12,199.99
FICA:             4,050.00       12,199.99      12,199.99
Work State:       4,050.00       12,199.99      12,199.99
Res. State:           0.00            0.00           0.00
County:               0.00            0.00           0.00
City:                 0.00            0.00           0.00
```

FIGURE 4-5 EasyBusiness Systems Employee Master Record

concise, and readable form. Reports are dated and numbered, and include headings which indicate the type of information contained in the report. Other important printed materials (e.g., financial reports, statements, checks and advices, order confirmations, and credit memos) can be custom formatted. An easy-to-use forms specification editor is included within each module for just this purpose.

The EasyBusiness Systems incorporates a thorough error-checking system. When an error is detected, the system displays an error message at the bottom of the screen. These messages are clear and complete, and lead the operator to quick, easy corrections. For additional help, an appendix in each manual gives comprehensive information about every error and its remedy.

There is one notable program idiosyncrasy, however, that should be mentioned. Normally, the EasyBusiness Systems maintains a scrupulous audit trail within each module. You are required to print out a complete proofing journal before posting—with one exception. Using the EasyPlus windowing system, you can transfer data from window to window, without being required to print out a hardcopy record of your transactions. Some accounting professionals may find this circumvention of the forced audit trail a serious flaw.

In conclusion, the EasyBusiness Systems' reputation as a state-of-the-art product certainly is well deserved. Menu organization and user-interface is logical and consistent, and the system's close integration and quick access to data are difficult to surpass. The package's top-notch documentation and support do everything possible to reduce and simplify learning problems. Since the setup time for an automated system inevitably costs more than the accounting software itself, this concern for streamlining the installation process results in substantial savings for the end-user. Given the system's proven track record, a wide variety of businesses could choose the EasyBusiness Systems and be confident of productive results.

Chapter 5

Surveying the Competition

This chapter contains critical evaluations of 12 integrated accounting systems, representing several of the leading products in the accounting software market. All of these systems feature the five basic accounting functions: General Ledger, Accounts Receivable, Accounts Payable, Inventory, and Payroll. Some provide additional accounting functions or offer compatibility with other applications software, like database management or word processing programs.

Along with the benchmark review, these evaluations will present you with a close look at some of the latest and most popular accounting systems currently in use. These products were selected for their ability to meet the basic needs required by most business users. As a group, they exemplify a diverse selection of accounting program styles and enhancements.

As you study the accounting systems in this chapter, you'll find a wide range of prices and sophistication. Some of these products are well-known best sellers, downsized from minicomputer accounting packages that have been around for a decade. Others are up-and-comers specifically written for the microcomputer environment, still trying to define and capture their share of the business market.

Presented alphabetically, each entry begins with a Fact File that contains the product name and publishing company, system requirements, program compatibility, and price tag. Compatible products, unless otherwise noted, are produced by the same publisher.

The system requirements statement includes the operating system(s), minimum memory, and disk storage. It also lists recommended equipment or peripherals, such as a specific printer. All of the products reviewed in this book were tested on an IBM PC-XT hard disk computer.

Compatibility refers to other software programs which also work with the reviewed product. For example, some publishers offer additional software products that can be linked together to share data files or to provide word processing functions for additional manipulation of your accounting information.

Price refers to the suggested retail, but it's not unusual to find significantly lower prices if you shop around.

After the brief Fact File, you'll find a basic review and evaluation of each accounting management system. The essential characteristics of each individual module are described at length, along with any outstanding strengths and weaknesses inherent in the program's design and handling.

The reviews also comment on intended markets, ease of use, and security. Documentation discussions tell you exactly what you can expect in terms of the user's manual, reference cards, keyboard templates, online help screens, and tutorials or sample lessons, if included. Good documentation is crucial in teaching you how to use an automated accounting system successfully.

The information provided in these reviews is based on test results from actual accounting business users who applied the evaluation criteria presented in Appendix A. In the chapter following this one, you'll find a comprehensive series of product comparison tables. For even more information on the products mentioned, see the directory of accounting management software publishers listed in Appendix B.

Although most of the language used in this part of the book has been explained earlier, you may find it helpful to consult the Glossary of Terms for quick and concise definitions.

The Accounting Partner II

COMPANY:	Star Software Systems
REQUIREMENTS:	PC-DOS, MS-DOS, CP/M-80, or CP/M-86; 128K; two disk drives or hard disk; 132-column printer or 80-column printer with compressed mode.
COMPATIBILITY:	Professional Time and Billing.
PRICES:	Modules not sold separately. Total system ($995); without Inventory ($795).

Star Software System's Accounting Partner II is one of the least expensive, full-featured, double-entry accounting systems on the market. Designed for small businesses, the system incorporates open item and balance forward accounting, six general ledger journals, and close integration all for under $1,000. Like systems three times the price, Accounting Partner II's modules can either stand alone or integrate with each other.

Accounting Partner II comes in a velcro-sealed plastic box about the size of a large dictionary. Inside are eight disks: two each for Accounts Receivable, Accounts Payable, and Payroll, and one each for General Ledger and Inventory. The package includes a bound, softback manual for every application, plus a separate installation guide for the entire system.

The manuals devote a chapter to each master menu function. These are broken down further into subsidiary menu selections, creating a logical path for you to follow while learning how the system operates. This good organization, however, could have been enhanced had the publisher included an index and a glossary of error messages.

The installation guide gives a complete explanation of scheduling and executing conversion from a manual to a computerized system. The guide also takes you through data entry for each application, and a useful section entitled "Cutting Over to Accounting Partner II" isolates the procedure for terminating the concomitant maintenance of your manual system—the last stage of your step into automation. In addition, the guide includes conversion checklists, worksheets for consolidating company information, and a detailed section on backup procedures.

Accounting Partner II's General Ledger allows simple entry of accounting transactions in six standard journals. The chart of accounts is quite flexible, and you can create budgets for up to 12 months. The master menu breaks main operations into five logical groups: chart of accounts maintenance, enter/sort/post transactions, print reports, end-of-period processing, and system initialization.

In addition to printing a series of standard reports, the G/L program also will generate budgeting reports—a bonus feature for such a low-priced system.

At the request of Accounting Partner users, Accounting Partner II's A/R module includes several new features and functions. The most notable addition is that of open item accounting—a necessity for any business that maintains a substantial inventory.

Another nice feature is the ability to identify accounts by number or name. This option, incidentally, is available throughout the system. Customer information maintained by the A/R module includes account number, name, sales and shipping addresses, accounting information, discounts, finance charge percentage, salesperson, type of account, resale status, multi-pricing codes, account terms reference number, credit limit, and auto-invoice amounts. You may list customer statistics in customer number order or alphabetical order.

After completing the invoice entry for an order, you may add discounts, sales tax, freight, and miscellaneous charges. At this point, you can print invoices, or batch them for printing at a later time. Invoices and statements are printed on standard NEBS (New England Business Systems) forms.

Details maintained for every order include sales order number, invoice terms, date shipped, F.O.B. point, and shipping method. You can use the item file provided by the A/R program for invoicing, and the system includes an item description and price per unit. Unfortunately, the A/R item file will not integrate with that of the Inventory module.

After you enter vendor and purchase order information, as well as payments and debits, the Accounts Payable module will retrieve all vendor activity information and print it on vendor lists, vendor worksheets, purchase orders, or internal management reports, at your discretion. These reports provide up-to-the-minute information in an easy-to-read and understandable format.

You can specify reports to contain a single account, an account range, or all accounts. The A/P module will also generate vendor lists, account statuses, accounts payable aging, purchase orders, and payment registers. In addition to the purchase order system, the A/P module maintains an item file that includes description and pricing information. This information has obvious utility when creating detailed purchase orders.

Accounting Partner II's Inventory module is designed for businesses that maintain finished goods inventories, such as wholesalers, distributors, and retailers. It maintains standard item information, and processes receipts, shipments, returns, and adjustments. The module also holds up to 12 months of historical inventory data for analysis.

The Inventory module contains a complete purchase ordering system for writing and tracking items, and it will support FIFO, LIFO, or moving average costing schemes. A costing file maintains such information as maximum cost, minimum cost, as well as most recent cost, thereby providing the basis for extensive analysis reports. You can instruct the module to print status reports, costing reports, valuation reports, transaction registers, movement reports, physical inventory worksheets, variance reports, and reorder reports.

The Payroll module contains all the functions necessary to meet the requirements of most small businesses. The employee file has separate fields for date hired, termination date, marital status, and miscellaneous comments, as well as wage and/or salary information. Hourly and salaried pay periods can be weekly, biweekly, semimonthly, or monthly. Time card information includes regular hours, overtime hours, double time hours, triple time hours, sick hours, vacation hours, tips, bonuses, commissions, miscellaneous income, exempt income, gross deductions, and two miscellaneous deductions.

The module offers the following standard reports: employee lists, payroll registers, employee pay histories, 941s, W-2s, tax deposit reports, and quarterly taxable earnings. You can print all of these reports in employee number order or in alphabetical order by name.

Not surprisingly, the Accounting Partner II lacks some features often found in higher-priced systems. For example, there is no help system to speak of, and none of the modules offers any internal security. Nonetheless, the system's ease of use and installation compare well with most competitors. If you don't expect your business to exceed the system's 1,000-account maximum any time soon, the Accounting Partner II may be able to give you a high degree of utility for the least amount of money.

BPI Accounting Series

COMPANY:	BPI Systems, Inc.
REQUIREMENTS:	PC-DOS or MS-DOS; 256K; two disk drives or hard disk; 80-column printer.
COMPATIBILITY:	Job Cost; Time Accounting; Church Management; Business Analyst; Information Management; Association Management; Speed Reading; Self-Training Series.
PRICES:	General Accounting ($595); Accounts Receivable ($595); Accounts Payable ($595); Inventory ($795); Payroll ($595). Total price: $3,175.

Conceived by the owner of a chain of grocery stores who wanted to computerize his accounting methods, BPI has held a healthy share of the microcomputer accounting market since the software was first released in 1982. BPI has expanded since that time into a family of software that meets an unusually wide range of business requirements.

The BPI system is menu driven and easy to use. The Data Entry and Maintenance menu in each module divides program options into three logical groupings: one for program functions, one for transaction entry, and a third for printing reports. Throughout the system, the first digit of a menu selection indicates the type of function it performs.

The entry system does not support cursor keys or line editing. This can make transaction entry a bit awkward. The back space key is the only editing key in the system. It will erase the character to the left of the cursor, or, if you're at the beginning of a field, it will move you to the previous field. As a compensation for this deficiency, the system lets you send all reports and listings to the screen before routing them to the printer, so you can preview your work before it turns into hardcopy.

One nice feature is a Queue menu that will let you enter transactions in several journals without having to return to the main menu. Usually an exclusive feature of large mainframe accounting systems, this allows you to set up a list of commands, or create a roster of reports to print out in any order you wish. While you take a break, the computer will perform your preset tally of instructions automatically.

A user-defined password up to six characters long acts as a gatekeeper for the entire system. BPI also guards the integrity of your data by generating complete audit trails—perhaps a little too complete. When you post transactions, the system prints out the entire ledger. If the ledger is long, and if you post your transactions several times a month, you're in for a time-consuming mountain of paperwork.

Although some functions, such as end-of-month processing, are accompanied by sketchy onscreen instructions, BPI does not really offer an online help system. Error handling, however, is quite good. BPI traps operating system errors and alerts you to their occurrence, and all errors conjure up a brief but adequate description of the error type. The "Solving Problems" section in each manual gives you all the information you are likely to need for corrective action.

In general, the manual that comes with every BPI module is sensibly written and well-illustrated. The authors liberally apply boldface print to augment their step-by-step, heading-by-heading tutorial style. All chapters provide an accounting overview that clarifies how the area of the program being discussed relates to the accounting system as a whole. A sample data disk sets you up for data entry and processing.

The introduction to each manual acquaints you with the general operation of your system's hardware, including a cogent explanation of the standard keyboard and how it relates to the software. The "Getting Started" chapter covers such subjects as installation and setup, making backup copies, and setting up system parameters. In addition to a list of error messages and explanations, the "Solving Problems" chapter includes a question-and-answer session that provides you with a way out of most common dilemmas.

The General Accounting module is a G/L package that supports up to 2,000 accounts—not an overly generous number. You can divide these accounts into four different ledger categories: general ledger, employees, vendors, and customers. Account codes are four digits long, and are grouped into current assets, fixed assets, other assets, current liabilities, long-term liabilities, capital, income, cost of sales, expenses, other income, other expenses, and income transfers. Each of these categories has a fixed numeric range that must be adhered to when setting up the chart of accounts. Within these ranges, the numeric sequence of account numbers determines the order in which accounts will be listed on the balance sheet.

You can set up a general journal for periodic posting of recurring entries, and generate the full range of standard reports. Because BPI is a month-to-month accounting system, however, there's no way to produce budgets, projections, or comparative statements.

The Accounts Receivable module supports both balance forward and open item accounting. It also handles four types of charge accounts, including those with revolving charges and fixed installment payments. Two levels of finance charges indicate the rate and the minimum balance for each level, and the package can automatically waive finance charges for specific customers. You can define the number of days in a billing period, and the month that marks the end of your fiscal year.

You can preset the default distribution of income to certain accounts, thereby saving time and improving accuracy by having the system suggest the account to which payment should be assigned. If so instructed, the system will apply payments automatically to outstanding invoices in open item accounts. At the end of an accounting period, you can process information to be transferred to the general ledger with a single command.

In addition to the standard ledgers, journals, schedules, and statements, the A/R module will print account analyses for all customers, selected customers, current past due accounts, year-to-date past due accounts, and accounts for which finance charges may be waived. You can also print past due notices, mailing labels, aged accounts receivable, and lists of repetitive charges and finance charges.

The BPI Accounts Payable module enters all transactions through a voucher system, resulting in efficient processing of a high volume of transactions for each accounting period, and superior control over tracking and posting. You may print checks automatically according to individual voucher, all open vouchers, or individual vendors.

This module supports both accrual and cash accounting—a useful feature if you operate your business on a cash basis. You can enter transactions at the time they occur to supply accurate cash requirements reports. Transactions are not posted to the expense accounts until payment is actually made. As in the A/R module, the system prompts you to post transactions to the default account.

The reports supplied by the A/P module provide the necessary information to manage vendor payments and plan cash requirements effectively. In addition to automatically printing checks, the system also will generate aged unpaid invoices, open vouchers, check registers, general ledger summaries, and vendor files and analyses.

You can establish up to 10 departments as profit centers in BPI's Inventory module. The package will record sales, cost of sales, and inventory overage and shrinkage information for each department. When the module is integrated with the A/R and Payable modules, transactions are recorded automatically for sales and purchase orders. Branch offices can write invoices from each location. Reports include income statements, sales journals, and supporting schedules. The package supports standard costing methods, tax exemptions, and a single sales tax amount.

The BPI system is a complete accounting series incorporating many useful features. Due in part to the selection of BASIC as a programming language, however, the system is not too speedy. During printing operations, the program spends as much time looking up and processing information as it does printing. Some users also may be put off by the slim four-digit account number, not to mention the overzealous audit trail (a simple posting journal would have sufficed).

On the other hand, the system has a reputation for dependability, and the proliferation of add-on modules is sure to please businesses with unique demands. If your company is quite small, BPI's General Accounting package may be all you need, since it includes the limited ability to handle receivables, payables, and payroll—more so than most stand-alone general ledgers. This system is a reliable industry standard, with enough attractive features and expandability to satisfy most users.

CYMA General Business System

COMPANY:	CYMA Corporation
REQUIREMENTS:	PC-DOS, MS-DOS, CP/M, MP/M, or CP/M-86; 64K; two disk drives or hard disk; 80-column printer.
COMPATIBILITY:	CYMA Professional Help, the Final Draft; CYMA Chiropractic; CYMA Dental; CYMA Client Accounting; CYMA Orthodontic; CYMA Medical; Shoe Box Accountant.
PRICES:	General Ledger ($795); Accounts Receivable ($795);Accounts Payable ($795); Inventory ($795); Payroll ($795). Total price: $2,995 (General Business System); $2,495 (General Business System without Inventory).

The CYMA Corporation develops and markets application software through dealers, distributors, CPA firms, and hardware manufacturers. In addition to the major accounting packages, CYMA offers a full array of vertical application packages. The accounting packages are designed for the company whose annual gross revenue is in the range of $100,000 to $25,000,000.

A special strength of the CYMA series is that all transactions are entered through a voucher system. This provides additional control over tracking and posting. The result is efficient processing of a high volume of transactions for each accounting period. This package is particularly attractive for companies that require detailed sales analysis reporting.

The system has superior password protection. Multilevel security codes are provided. This includes the use of passwords and security codes for access to certain individual functions. Errors are trapped at the time of input in the form of account verifications and valid date checking.

Documentation is provided in a three-ring binder. Many screens are illustrated in detail, and their functions are explained fully. A chapter on visualizing the system provides a good overview and familiarizes the user with the terms used throughout the package. The manual includes handy tabs to separate the basic areas, but the very small index does not provide much help. Support is provided by the dealer, and CYMA provides training through its dealer network only. A sample data base is not included.

CYMA's General Ledger stores journal transactions and job cost entries with complete audit trails. The software provides up to 26 different user-defined financial statement formats, and produces a comprehensive range of financial reports for screen display or printing. The audit trail is generated in the form of listings and entry journals that reflect accounts altered in any way.

The G/L system includes one- to eight-digit, user-defined account numbers for complete job cost flexibility. The program will allow 13-month accounting. As journal entries are being made, the G/L module will alert you to out-of-balance entries or erroneous account numbers.

Variance reports illustrate dollar and/or percentage variance, and ongoing display of batch, journal, and ledger totals. Other capabilities include trial balance and fund flow worksheets, specific budget and/or account updates, optional automatic generation of recurring and/or reversing entries, and the option of closing accounts into one specific account.

The CYMA Accounts Receivable module includes a screen display of all transactions and listings for online access to information. CYMA's A/R package will maintain balance forward, open item, or contract long-term receivable accounts concurrently. Payment coupons can be printed for contract customers. The A/R system prints complete audit trails for all transactions, generates recurring entries automatically, calculates finance charges and discounts individually for customers, and automatically posts to proper offset accounts when integrated with the G/L module. In addition, it produces sales receipts and day sheets along with year-to-date sales and finance charge reports, and analyzes sales by date, product line, or department.

The Accounts Payable module includes print and display options for all reports. The reports offer information useful for money management and calculation of future discounts and penalties. Four user-defined columns show variable aging of payables (past or future due). This allows you to gauge cash flow and enter partial payments to reflect the new balance in the account.

The A/P module also allows automatic recurring entries. Complete invoice detail can be sorted and subtotaled in many different ways. Cash totals can be displayed on the screen by invoice and batch.

Finance charge reports show when discounts or penalties can be applied, along with the percentage, dollar amount, and the number of days remaining either to take advantage of discounts or avoid penalties. Options to select invoices prior to check writing, voucher checks with or without invoice detail, and a check register that maintains broken check sequences and voided checks are also included.

The CYMA Inventory package is a complete inventory control and order entry system that handles multilevel bills of materials, sales and purchase order entry, back order tracking, sub-assemblies, and the tracking of finished goods in multiple locations. It is designed for small manufacturing or wholesale operations, and can be integrated with other CYMA packages.

No materials management experience is necessary to operate the system. Features include user-defined part number lengths (from 4 to 30 alphanumeric characters), five valuation methods (LIFO, FIFO, weighted average, moving average, specific item), and reports that can be displayed on the screen for instant online access to information. Transaction journals of all sales and purchase orders are printed to provide an audit trail and monitor input errors. Up to four price levels per part are provided, along with automatic markups and price calculations to ensure accurate pricing.

A wide variety of reports can be printed to show sales analysis for inventory control. These include reports that deal with amount and percentage of gross margin, total revenue, and cost-of-goods sold. The reports can be printed by item, product category, or department. An overstockage report helps minimize inventory costs by flagging and totaling overstocked items. A physical worksheet sorted by bin number, location, vendor, or part (with or without quantities), makes physical inventory easy, fast, and accurate. An inventory valuation report, using any one of 10 price/cost levels, can be printed for up-to-the-minute inventory value.

The multi-state Payroll package automatically calculates gross pay, tax withholdings, deductions or allowances, and net pay for all employees. The module can handle regular, overtime, and double time hours, varying pay scales per employee, and can integrate to the General Ledger for complete job cost capabilities.

The package's features include the ability to handle hourly wages, salaries, or tips for employees at individualized payroll cycles and pay scales. It allows you to create tax tables for any federal, state, county, or city. Automatic tax calculations also are supported. You can create up to 26 different deductions or pay allowances, with eight apiece per employee.

The Payroll module prints labor analysis reports by account or job. The report information includes employee, hours, rate, and total dollars spent. The module will print verification of entries before posting and printing checks, maintain a check register, and identify broken check sequences or voided checks. It also contains a complete audit trail of changes in all Payroll data files, and a control feature that stores 941 payroll information.

The CYMA accounting series is easily installed. Most system operations are very responsive except for sorting and some file operations. Input verification for date and account code accuracy is performed, and the operator is re-prompted if the information is invalid—although a specific error message is not given. Instead, an instruction line is presented at the bottom of each screen showing the options available when calling for reports. An editing system is not supported, making corrections difficult. You can move to the previous field, however, if you catch the mistake before you complete the entire entry.

On the whole, CYMA General Business System has several unique attributes, especially the wide range of detailed analytical reports. This is a full-featured system, and users who would prefer to save themselves the cost of a hard disk may find its low memory requirements particularly attractive.

Champion Business Accounting Software

COMPANY:	Champion Software Corporation
REQUIREMENTS:	PC-DOS, MS-DOS, CP/M-80, or CP/M-86; 128K; two disk drives or hard disk; 80-col. printer with form feed capability.
COMPATIBILITY:	Password Security System; Freeway; dBASE II (Ashton-Tate).
PRICES:	General Ledger ($595); Accounts Receivable ($595); Accounts Payable ($595); Inventory ($595); Payroll ($595). Total price: $2,975.

Champion Business Accounting Software is an easy-to-use accounting system written in the popular database programming language, dBASE II. This language offers uniform file management and the luxury of an accounting package that takes up little disk space; if you buy the system as an integrated package, you'll find that all five modules are packed onto three disks.

Champion markets its system, either in separate modules or as an integrated whole, with a 30-day, money-back guarantee. During this trial period, you are limited to 200 transactions per module. Champion requires that you register to get the security code that breaks these transaction limits, thereby formalizing your purchase. Once you're up and running, Champion offers phone support at $250 for one year, with a five-hour maximum limit.

The context-sensitive help system included in each package is an excellent reference tool. Asking for assistance is as simple as hitting a "?" key, at which point a window appears containing remarkably complete information about the routine in progress. Invalid data entry is greeted by equally complete error messages—not just error numbers. Champion also supplies a "recover" disk for catastrophic errors, such as those resulting from an overflowing disk or a power outage.

To expedite setup and other basic procedures, Champion includes a program called Easyup to help you install the software, allocate data files, change disk assignments, and close the books at year-end. Easyup is true to its name, and it's particularly useful when calculating estimated storage requirements.

Two separate manuals comprise the system's documentation: the Installation & Operations Guide, and the Reference Guide, which takes you through the system's various features and functions. The Reference Guide includes instructions for converting each accounting application from a manual to an automated system, and on the whole, explanations are lucid, concise, and logically formatted. The different sections of the manuals are separated by tabs for quick information access.

Champion is a full double-entry accounting system; General Ledger balance must be maintained at all times, or you cannot complete an entry. Transaction journals supply the audit trail. Champion uses the standard dBASE II editing system, which affords substantial cursor movement and some field editing functions. The escape key lets you abort any procedure in progress and return to the previous onscreen menu.

Unlike most automated accounting systems, Champion does not support the batch entry mode. This means transactions acquired from any module are posted automatically to G/L at the time of entry, and you must go through the arduous process of entering compensating transactions to correct entry errors. On the other hand, this also ensures a pristine audit trail, completely current account balances, and financial statements that immediately reflect the entry of any relevant transaction. You are also spared time-consuming sorting, posting, and end-of-month closing procedures, and you can leave any or all accounting periods open throughout the fiscal year.

The General Ledger supplies listings for any month, any account or range of accounts, and cash disbursements and receipt journals for each individual account, date, or range of accounts. A user-defined code allows both departmental and/or cost accounting. The financial reporting function provides fixed formats for income statements, trial balance sheets, balance sheets, and subsidiary financial statement schedules. The reports may be printed in individual, combined, or consolidated form.

Champion's Accounts Receivable module supports both balance forward and open item billing, and you have nine customer discount levels from which to choose. If you run the Inventory module and the A/R module in tandem, seven inventory classifications can interact with the discount levels, providing a whopping 63 discount combinations, one of the largest in microcomputer accounting software.

A point-of-sale invoicing feature provides running cash drawer balances, perpetual inventory reports, and customer updates after each invoice. Debit and credit memos can be tied to specific invoices as well. Invoices may be printed by order number sequence, customer number, or shipping date order, and both back orders and open orders are supported.

The Accounts Payable module includes a complete purchase order system. You can generate purchase order vouchers to help control the purchasing of new products and services, and both cash and accrual accounting methods are supported. When you make payments and print checks, the package updates the cash disbursements journal and other journals as required. Discounts can be computed by percentage or by flat dollar amounts.

Reports generated by either the A/R or A/P modules may be printed or viewed onscreen. These reports include customer lists, sales journals, and detail aged trial balances in A/R. In A/P, reports include vendor lists, discount and potential finance charge reports, and a check register with itemized voided checks. Sales analysis reports may be broken down by sales representative or inventory item number. Sales tax reports can be prepared by tax code or date. The A/P aging reports can greatly assist with planning cash requirements.

The Inventory module maintains inventory automatically by sales or by purchases. Inventory items may be arranged in product groups, subgroups, or departments. The weighted average method determines the costing of inventory, and a detail item file holds all the basic information for inventory record keeping. If you integrate the A/R and A/P modules, you can maintain additional sales and purchasing information. A full range of reports may be printed by this module to manage your inventory effectively, including an inventory master list, inventory activity reports, inventory planning reports, reorder reports, and adjustments journals.

Champion's Payroll module offers a complete set of features that meet the requirements of most employers. You may compute paychecks for weekly, biweekly, semimonthly, or monthly periods. Hours can be entered on any basis, including minutes or decimal hours. The program supports overtime and double time, as well as various other pay types.

You may print or view onscreen a prepayments audit list before actually processing the payroll. At the end of a given pay period, you can produce paychecks for one employee, a range of employees, or all employees. Tax tables for the 50 states, Washington D.C., and Puerto Rico are included.

You can perform cost appraisal by job or department based upon labor expenses. A complete set of payroll reports is provided, including 941s, 940s, state unemployment information, and W-2s. A comprehensive listing for each employee shows all transactions within the current year.

Champion does have some minor liabilities. The system creates a wide variety of reports, but their appearance is not particularly attractive, and your options for dressing them up are restricted to simple justification and centering of headings. Also, users who are partial to 13-month accounting may be turned away by Champion's decision to leave out this option.

These deficiencies, however, are outweighed by Champion's many positive features. The software verifies all account number and date entries, and the data recovery disk offers an extremely simple procedure for rebuilding data that otherwise would be lost. Report generation relies on a coding structure that allows you to create reports reflecting a single accounting parameter. These can be quite specific—e.g., a report that shows all payroll records by shift. Since Champion updates data on entry, rather than waiting until after posting, all reports are up-to-the-minute.

Overall, Champion Business Accounting Software is one of the easiest and most responsive integrated systems to operate. The context-sensitive help system is uniquely thorough, and it refers you to appropriate page numbers in the manual. No limit, except disk space, is placed on the number of entries in any document. As an added bonus, users with dBASE II expertise may order file structure specifications from the manufacturer to expand the package's already versatile reporting features. Although not as well known as some of its counterparts, Champion's flexibility and ease of use have established it as a formidable competitor in the accounting software market.

Hardisk Accounting Series

COMPANY:	Great Plains Software
REQUIREMENTS:	PC-DOS, MS-DOS, CP/M; 128K; hard disk; 132-column printer or 80-column printer with compressed mode.
COMPATIBILITY:	Job Cost; Report Maker; Rapid Transfer.
PRICES:	General Ledger ($595); Accounts Receivable ($595); Accounts Payable ($595); Inventory Management ($595); Payroll ($595). Multiuser versions are $795 each.

The Hardisk Accounting Series, from Great Plains Software, is a menu-driven integrated program written in PASCAL. The system's menu provides a set of general utilities that make the operation of the modules easy. This includes a backup and restore function, a system for maintaining passwords, and hardware configuration procedures. A strong, multilevel security system is offered, which can restrict access for different functions to different operators. The A/R module has a flexible scheme for recording partial payments on accounts.

Before installation, you must determine the number of accounts that will be contained in each of the modules. This number is used in a formula to determine the number of blocks required for file allocation. Since the software must run on a hard disk system, however, general operation is good. You may move from one accounting function to another very easily.

The user manuals are complete and easy to follow. A thorough explanation of each accounting procedure and its functions is included for each module. Step-by-step instructions make most procedures simple to follow. Common errors are trapped at entry time, and account number and date verifications are performed to guarantee integrity. A single level of password protection is provided, and a full set of audit trails is generated by the system. Posting journals are printed at the necessary intervals.

The General Ledger can maintain up to 32,766 accounts with up to 999 profit centers. A running total of debits and credits is tabulated automatically. The system will not post entries that are out of balance. Beginning and ending dates can be shown on all financial statements, along with all profit centers.

Statements can be printed by profit center, and sales ratios can be computed as a percentage of the company's total revenues. Financial statements can compare actual financial statement results with last year's figures or budget figures. Budget figures can be included on reports, along with last year's figures.

The chart of accounts controls the structure for the entire G/L package. The account number consists of the main account code, an extension of the sub-account code, and a departmental code. Up to 30 characters provide the account description, which also is used by the financial reporting module. A financial statement code controls how the account is handled during report printing. This identifier notes whether the account is a balance sheet or profit and loss account, how it will be sorted on the financial statements, and whether it is a header, subheader, total, or subtotal account.

Since this is a time-consuming system to install, a thorough understanding of how a general ledger operates is extremely useful. Obtaining financial statements in the style you desire will most likely require some assistance from your accountant.

Budget amounts and last year's account totals are maintained for the production of comparative statements. A 13-period accounting cycle is not supported.

Transaction entries are recorded in a batch mode. A transaction includes the account number, date, debit and credit amount, a source indicator, a description, and a journal entry number.

The report section of the G/L generates a standard chart of accounts listing, transaction registers, edit listings, detail account listings, a trial balance worksheet, and a transaction cross-reference listing.

Financial statements are limited to a profit and loss statement and a balance sheet. Profit and loss statements may be printed by department, can contain a total or subtotal of sales, and include year-to-date figures. A comparative budget statement also may be printed. Changes in financial position are not included.

Accounts Receivable will handle up to 32,000 customers, although the documentation states that only 3,000 can be handled "efficiently." Users can add, change, and delete a customer at any time, but are not allowed to delete a customer with a balance. The A/R program allows for either balance forward or open item handling of each customer, and will check a customer's balance against credit terms automatically. The system allows for posting to any G/L account, and invoices can be distributed to 16 different G/L accounts.

Special features of the A/R program include the ability to enter full or partial payments and the capacity to apply payment to all invoices or just specific invoices. The system also allows you to apply finance charges to overdue accounts, and it automatically identifies slow payers. This aids cash flow situations within the business itself. The traditional aging periods of 30, 60, and 90 days can be used, or you can define your own. An A/R account file inquiry screen allows you to check quickly the status of any customer. The open file reference summarizes the numbers and dollar amounts of balances, invoices, service charges, debit memos, payments, returns, finance charges, and totals the net amount of receivables. In addition, suggested posting accounts in A/R make data entry faster.

Accounts Payable can handle up to 29 fields of data, depending on disk capacity. This module can enter non-discountable amounts and automatically will calculate early payment discounts. Transaction entries can be distributed to 16 G/L accounts, and full or partial payments can be made on any open item invoice. Payments also can be withheld, or made by handwritten checks.

Other features of the A/P module include the ability to change due dates or discount dates on specific vouchers, defer by voucher or by date, and undefer deferred payments. An immediate screen inquiry of vendors on file is available through the vendor list program.

Users will rely on the A/P open file reference as a quick summary of the numbers and dollar amounts of invoices, prepaid vouchers, payments, partial payments, and deferred payments. Also, the A/P onscreen query system includes a listing of each outstanding invoice, aging by user-defined aging periods, balance, company contact person, and phone number. A convenient cash due summary report graphically displays an invoice aging table that shows when discounts are available, making cash management easier.

The basic vendor record contains a service address for those vendors who have a different address for returns or orders. A UPS zone code also is provided along with a default shipping method. Two G/L default distribution accounts are provided, thus simplifying transaction entry. A field is supplied to enter minimum order requirements. Running totals are also maintained for amounts billed/paid, discounts taken/lost, and finance charges.

Transactions are recorded using the batch method. Voucher numbers are assigned automatically after the first voucher number is entered. Discounts may be handled by percentage or dollar amounts. A fixed non-discount amount also can be entered. Invoice vouchers are distributed to G/L accounts, with default accounts presented first for amount entry. Additional accounts may be entered as required.

A full set of A/P reports may be printed by the system. These include vendors listed alphabetically, by vendor number, by contact person, by state, by zip code, and by telephone number. A detail aged trial balance shows all accounting detail for the current period.

Cash requirement planning is assisted by payments due and requirements report as well as a deferred items report. A pre-check register may be printed prior to actual check printing. A vendor analysis report provides summaries by vendor of year-to-date activity and average amount of invoice, as well as the percent of total payables activity.

The Inventory module has a recommended limit of 6,000 part numbers, depending on disk capacity. Inventory items can be identified and reported by six user-defined categories. Five price levels and three quantity price breaks are available, and four pricing methods can be used. Price breaks can be set for each item, and orders meeting the quantity price break point are given the right price level automatically. Serial numbers also can be tracked, and quantities can be maintained with zero, one, or two decimal places of accuracy. Cost information can be maintained with two, three, or four decimal places of accuracy. Inventory evaluation is performed automatically using either FIFO, LIFO, or weighted moving average, and two substitution items are suggested automatically for out-of-stock items. Promotion information is maintained on a per-item basis, and promotion discounts can be set at a dollar or percent amount.

The point-of-sale "cash register" program allows the inventory to be updated automatically as sales are made. This program handles cash and credit sales and returns, and automatically prints a sales slip or invoice for each transaction, as well as allowing you to tailor sales slips to individual needs. When integrated with the A/R module, the point-of-sale program can access existing customer information, as well as add new customers.

The Payroll module calculates the payroll deductions, includes all state tax tables, and accommodates payroll accounting in all of the 50 states.

Payroll is calculated by hourly pay, salary, incentive, flat rates, and commissions. Weekly, biweekly, semi-monthly, monthly, quarterly, semi-annual, and annual payroll periods are supported. User-defined automatic overtime calculation is included, and up to 999 user-defined categories are possible. All deduction categories are computed separately, and reports can be generated from them.

Wages for one employee may be distributed among five departments, and department changes are handled easily. Job cost is reported by job name. Total hours, as well as total dollar amounts of the payroll, are reported for each department. Advanced earned income credit payments are handled, and the employer's federal unemployment income report is calculated. Payroll checks are written by the system, but manual checks can not be accommodated.

The Payroll module can maintain up to 32,000 employees, although 250 is the recommended limit. It prepares information for 941s and reports overtime for each pay period. Standard recurring deductions are maintained by the system along with employee earnings history, employment date, and the reason for termination.

Special features found in the Payroll package are the ability to track piecework for gross pay. This is calculated on a per piece completed basis. Tracking tips, personal leave, funeral leave, administrative leave, leave without pay, jury duty, and profit sharing also can be effected. Tip handling is broken down further by tips deemed wages and paid tips deemed wages.

The overall performance of Great Plains' accounting products is adequate. The many features found within the individual modules should be evaluated for your particular type of business. Cost center record keeping abilities are among the packages' strongest features. If you require these features, then this may be the package for you.

IBM Business Management Series

COMPANY:	IBM Corporation
REQUIREMENTS:	PC-DOS; 256K; hard disk; 132-column printer.
COMPATIBILITY:	Order Entry Edition; Personal Decision Series; BMS Computer-Based Training packages (available for each module).
PRICES:	General Ledger ($695); Accounts Receivable ($695); Accounts Payable ($695); Inventory Accounting ($695); Payroll ($695). Total Price: $3,475.

If you're acquainted with the feature-laden, high-volume character of minicomputer accounting, IBM's Business Management Series (BMS) will look very familiar. Derived from accounting software originally created for IBM's System/23, System/34, and System/36 minicomputers, this system is designed for mid-sized companies with detailed accounting requirements. Nothing has been lost in translation from mini to micro, including the software's size.

Written in BASIC and replete with functions, the programs that make up the accounting system are quite large and require a hard disk system. The General Ledger, in fact, takes up nine disks alone. If you decide to automate several accounting functions, and plan to enter over 1,000 transactions a month, you may require more than a 10-megabyte hard disk. In other words, the BMS package really should be run on the IBM PC-AT.

Size considerations aside, the BMS programs offer a number of outstanding features. The context-sensitive help system is particularly thorough; if you move the cursor to virtually any entry field and press the F1 function key, you get a complete explanation of that field. Considering that there may be dozens of fields on a single screen, this is indeed an impressive online aid.

The system safeguards the integrity of your data in several ways. Each module may be assigned a separate password that will restrict access to authorized personnel. The system also generates an exhaustive audit trail, and frequently reminds you to make backup files.

The BMS system comes with first-rate documentation. Each module includes a profusely illustrated manual that walks you through system operations in a step-by-step format. One appendix describes in detail how to collect and organize your accounting information to prepare for input, and another helps you batch your transaction data by supplying a set of entry forms included for the purpose. Sample data and exercises give you valuable practice.

Appendices also give comprehensive explanations of error messages, show you how to integrate the system with IBM's Personal Decision Series, and provide a prototype chart of accounts. Each manual contains a thorough index, and a laminated quick reference card supplies basic keyboard commands.

To help you through those inevitable rough spots, IBM offers an extensive telephone support program. This includes 90 days worth of free phone support, and an extended support subscription plan for $225 a year per module. You also can purchase telephone assistance for $40 a call, or pay $180 for a prepaid package of five calls.

The General Ledger allows you to set up as many as five special journals, complete with special columns for tracking funds to specific accounts. Journal entries include a source code, posting date, account number, debit or credit amount, reference number, description, and reference date. The G/L also assigns journal numbers that allow you to trace entries back to their source.

The system supports the batch entry mode, and you may list and edit transactions before posting. If you choose to enter encumbrances, the G/L module will print out an encumbrance posting list. At specified intervals, the module will also enter and post recurring journal entries, whether they are simple debits and credits using fixed amounts, or debits and credits that are calculated from various combinations of account balances, percentages, and fixed amounts.

Standard reports generated by the G/L module include separate journals for the General Ledger, special journals, a trial balance which may be listed in a worksheet format, and the detailed G/L listing. The detailed G/L listing may be printed with a number of options controlling format, content, and range of accounts. A wide array of comparative statements gives you the kind of up-to-date financial information that makes automated accounting worthwhile.

The A/R module allows you to enter invoice transactions directly, or pick them up from the Order Entry module (if installed). You may print selected invoices for one customer or a range of customers, and process invoices with future dates. IBM includes three sales tax categories, and totals for orders, sales, and cost of goods sold. Customers may have their own specified payment terms and late charges, and the option of balance forward or open item accounting.

You may define up to five columns for tracking sales, cash receipts, and adjustment entries. This very useful feature also provides specific types of transaction tracking that may be unique to your business.

The detail receivables ledger offers a choice of four adjustable aging periods. You may format the printout of accounts on this report by customer range, account balances, and aging periods. The last page of the report, which may be printed out by itself, shows the totals for all accounts printed. Like all of the subsidiary modules, the A/R package collects, summarizes, and transfers transaction information to the General Ledger.

The A/P package handles payables on an accrual basis. Vendor analysis reports allow you to determine key purchase volumes and discounts taken or lost for the current and previous year. The reports also show the total number of invoices received, and may be printed for one, all, or a specified range of vendors. A cash requirements report shows each invoice to be paid and each credit to be taken. The report also shows balance due, the amount you plan to pay, the discount you plan to take, and the net payment.

You can set up purchase and cash disbursement journals according to your company's specific needs, and up to five columns may be defined for special accounts. Invoices, credit memos, prepaid invoices, and check reversals are all easily handled, and you can select payment based on a due date or by individual invoice. You may also make partial payments on invoices or take partial credits on credit memos.

The Payroll module supports both hourly and salaried payroll processing. Individual earnings can be taxed for up to three taxing jurisdictions, and payroll may be processed on a weekly, biweekly, semimonthly, or monthly basis. The module will calculate gross and net pay, and track federal income tax, social security, state and local taxes, state disability insurance, federal unemployment tax, state unemployment insurance, and earned income credit. You may track multiple state and local taxes for as many states as you define.

A special feature tracks tips in a number of categories. These classifications include tips taxed, tips not taxed, total tips reported, total tips allocated, and tips deemed as wages. The Payroll also handles multiple miscellaneous deductions and benefits. IBM supplies tax registers which summarize state, local, and federal taxes. A worker's compensation worksheet provides all the details required to calculate your insurance liability.

The Payroll package produces a wide variety of reports. You can print earnings statements after payroll is calculated, and a payroll register shows each employee with all deductions and benefits. A distribution journal summarizes all transactions for automatic transfer to the General Ledger.

This review gives but a brief summary of the powerful features found in the BMS package. The system's size, though, makes it a bit slow, and the fact that the A/R and A/P modules do not interface with the Inventory Accounting module is a definite drawback. If your company is not accounting intensive, a smaller system might serve you better.

If your business is medium- to large-sized and generates a high volume of diverse accounting information, the Business Management Series may be for you. IBM covers all the bases—at a cost of $95 per application, you can even order training modules that augment the already generous documentation and help systems. Attention to detail is the great strength here. The IBM Business Management Series is, to say the least, an enormous, versatile, and thorough system.

Open Systems Accounting Software

COMPANY:	Open Systems, Inc.
REQUIREMENTS:	PC-DOS, MS-DOS, CP/M, or M/PM; 128K; hard disk; 80-column printer.
COMPATIBILITY:	Fixed Assets; Sales Order Processing; Purchase Order Processing; Job Cost; Report Writer.
PRICES:	General Ledger ($695); Accounts Receivable ($695); Accounts Payable ($695); Inventory ($695); Payroll($695). Total Price: $3,475.

Open Systems Accounting Software was developed originally for minicomputers in 1976. In 1978 it was adapted for CP/M. The software has many features for medium-sized companies, and the system's integration is excellent. The modules perform well together, especially when performing job costing functions—an area where many other microcomputer accounting systems fall short.

The system provides a strong accounting base for companies with many divisions or departments, and may be used in a multiuser environment. A special package called Report Writer lets you create custom reports from the accounting database. The possibilities inherent in the Report Writer module are virtually limitless. Any organization that needs its accounting information sorted, selected, and presented in a special way, will find this module extremely useful.

A series of passwords is provided to make the program available only to authorized personnel. User IDs can be set up to restrict access to some users and some areas, allowing one person to enter data, and someone else to process the information.

Transactions are checked at entry time for validity and proper content, and a full set of journals are printed, providing a complete audit trail.

Support generally is handled through the dealer network. However, phone support may be obtained directly from Open Systems for $1.95 per minute. Annual support for one module runs $195 per year; for all five modules, the rate is $725 per year.

The programs are written in BASIC, and the source code is provided. The code is well structured and consistent in design. Should you decide to modify the original program, the necessary information is here.

The documentation for Open Systems is very complete. An index provides quick location of any topic. Detailed explanations are provided, leaving the user with very little room for confusion. A full complement of reports is listed and described, as well as many examples of operations. The manuals are lucid, visually attractive, and accessible.

A separate manual is provided to guide system installation and setup. Still, installation of this system does require careful consideration, and it's probably best handled by a dealer familiar with Open Systems.

The G/L package handles actual, budget, and last-year data, and accommodates up to 13 accounting periods within a year. The chart of accounts numbers can be up to 12 digits long, and journal entries to the G/L carry both an eight-digit reference number and a 25-character description.

Clearing and closing accounts at the end of a period or consolidating accounts from several companies is accomplished automatically. When accounts are cleared and closed, costs are allocated to all departments in a company, step by step, until a more accurate picture of the company's finances merge. Multiple-company accounts are consolidated in a similar manner.

G/L reports are in standard formats, and you can generate custom income statement and balance sheet reports. Listings from the G/L are sorted and summarized and provide an adequate audit trail.

The Accounts Receivable module tracks funds received from customers on a balance forward or open item basis, or both. In the balance forward mode, a single balance due from a customer is maintained on a current basis, as well as a 30/60/90/120-day basis. The open item mode captures and maintains individual invoice balances and requires that cash payments be applied against these individual invoices.

The A/R package offers a fair amount of flexibility in report printing. Ranges for many categories can be specified, and reports are sorted by category number. For example, an open order report includes any designated range of customers, inventory, or job numbers. The program can generate a sales history report by customer, salesperson, job, invoice, product category, and inventory. Transactions also can be listed in detail or in summary.

Cash flow analysis is made easier with a report that uses aged customer balances to estimate the incoming cash from customer payments. These reports, coupled with the A/P aging report, provide you with information needed for accurate financial planning.

The A/P package competently records and manages invoices received and payments made. A special feature is the availability of a temporary vendor in which one-time invoices are recorded in the system, but not the A/P master file. Most other systems require that all vendors have an established account.

A/P integrates with the G/L, Inventory, and Job Cost modules, and disbursements are assigned to specific jobs and phases within a job. These disbursements can be assigned to cost codes, designating them as material, equipment, overhead, or other categories. Tax and freight costs are tracked separately, and you may schedule up to three payments to be made against an invoice.

The Inventory module effectively tracks item quantity and cost. Each stocked item is assigned an item number along with a description. Stock also can be assigned a user-defined category, a location, and a price code. For each item, the system maintains the quantity in stock committed to sales orders and purchase orders, and computes the remaining quantity. A vendor number also can be specified for each item and tied to desired minimum and maximum levels of stock. Inventory may be valued by LIFO, FIFO, or moving average cost.

A number of basic inventory reports is available, as well as management reports that sort and list sales by date of last sale and by descending sales volume. The package also produces an inventory report that indicates how fast an item is selling relative to the quantity on hand.

The Payroll module calculates federal, state, and other taxes, along with earned income credit and unemployment compensation. Five additional pay and deduction tables are available for voluntary deductions and miscellaneous pay schedules. In addition to standard payroll reports, the module will generate worksheets necessary to meet the filing requirements for 941s and W-2s.

In summary, Open Systems Accounting Software is a full-featured family of products. Program operation is simple and straightforward. The comprehensive documentation and excellent program design make this package one of the best accounting software systems available for microcomputers.

Peachtree Business Accounting System

COMPANY:	Peachtree Software, Inc.
REQUIREMENTS:	PC-DOS, MS-DOS, or CP/M; 128K; two disk drives or hard disk; 132-column printer.
COMPATIBILITY:	Fixed Assets; Job Cost; Sales Invoicing; PeachText; PeachCalc; List Manager (requires Access Pak).
PRICES:	General Ledger ($595); Accounts Receivable ($595); Accounts Payable ($595); Inventory Control ($595); Payroll ($595). Total price: $2,975.

Peachtree Software has been around as long as any microcomputer accounting software vendor. With so much experience, it's small wonder the company's business accounting package is among the easiest to use. The system is kind to bookkeepers without much computer experience, and user interface procedures are consistent throughout the modules. One special feature found in the Peachtree system is a program that backs up your data automatically during end-of-month processing.

All menu selections are made by entering a two-letter code, which may seem a bit primitive compared to systems with one-key selection. If you make a mistake, you must acknowledge an error message and re-enter your selection.

A limited editor is present in all of the modules. This includes the ability to jump to the next or previous field, and to the beginning or end of the current field. The back space key serves as a character-by-character delete function. No online help system is provided.

Control reports are generated automatically by the individual modules in the Peachtree system to provide complete audit trails. If the system is operated as an integrated accounting system, the individual modules print an end-of-period G/L report summarizing all transactions that will be transferred to the G/L system.

Installation of the system is accomplished by carefully following the setup instructions in the manual. The person installing the software for the first time should have a working knowledge of the computer operating system, and extreme care should be taken with the factory masters. Once you configure them, they may not be altered again without Peachtree's support.

Program operations are detailed in the user manual in a step-by-step fashion. A set of sample data files is provided with each module, and a special chapter (called "A Little Practice") gives you some hands-on experience before you actually enter your own information into the books. The exercises in the practice section take you through the most common accounting functions. You can practice entering and deleting information and accounts, learn the special functions of the keyboard, and make corrections.

A section on "Setting Up the Module" explains the options that a particular module offers, as well as showing you how to set up your initial accounts and enter opening balances. This is one of the most important sections in the manual. It defines terms and conventions used throughout the documentation, and explores reports and their requirements.

The glossaries included in each manual contain both general computer and accounting terms. An ample number of screens is shown, as well as a selection of report reproductions. Appendices contain error messages, input forms, a chart for calculating disk requirements, and technical information regarding file structures. A quick reference guide is provided that includes definitions and descriptions of the most common procedures.

Error messages are displayed when an invalid activity or system error has occurred. The most common of these are operator errors, such as invalid entry of dates or account numbers. Most errors require a simple acknowledgment of the error, such as pressing the enter key. Some error messages ask a "Yes/No?" question to recover from the error, while others contain only a cryptic error number. These numbered errors tend to be more serious, and require you to refer to the error appendix.

The G/L package maintains the chart of accounts and each account's activity. Information can be entered directly into the G/L or obtained from any of the other Peachtree accounting modules. Transaction details are maintained for one month, and monthly account totals are maintained for up to 24 accounting periods for comparative statements. This system does not allow for 13 fiscal periods in one year.

The chart of accounts must be laid out with care. Account numbers must lie within certain ranges to identify the category to which they belong. Categories include assets, liabilities, income, and expenses. Reports generated by the system are produced in account code order. Therefore, you must arrange your chart of accounts in the same order that you want your reports presented.

Accounts may contain actual entries or they may be control accounts. Control accounts represent headings, subtotals, or grouping controls on the financial statements. Grouped accounts make it possible to have a single line of a financial statement represent a range or group of account activity, without actually listing the individual account balances. Transaction registers provide listings of entries grouped by either account number or source code and reference number.

The Peachtree A/R module offers a full set of account management features. It prints invoices, statements, and aging reports, and maintains customer account information, sales tax, and the accounting detail for the G/L.

One feature found in this module—and missing in many other receivable systems—is a complete invoicing system. This includes 80-character item descriptions, quantity ordered, quantity shipped, unit price, line extensions, freight, tax, service charges, deposits, and discounts. Finance charges may be calculated on a daily balance or on period-ending balances.

Customer transactions are tracked through the invoicing systems. Customer summary statistics include name, address, phone, tax rate, current balance, balance forward, date and amount of last debit and credit, automatic billing amount, year-to-date sales, and year-to-date payments.

In addition to a complete file maintained on each vendor, the A/P package helps determine which invoices to pay by due date, by discount date, or by certain cash requirements. A manual selection of individual invoices also can be made. The system will print a number of detail cash requirements reports by due date or discount date. Checks and advices can be printed automatically, and aging reports will classify transactions into six time periods.

The Peachtree Inventory Control module keeps track of individual inventory items as transactions occur. The system provides detailed information, such as year-to-date activity, price, balance on hand, physical inventory counts, total sales figures, cost-of-sales, and profit margins.

You can maintain inventory control information in summary form or in extensive detail to provide a comprehensive audit trail of inventory activity. Three pricing levels are available for volume purchase discounts, and standard or average costing methods are offered.

The Inventory module's reporting function generates control reports for all entry programs to ensure accurate audit trails. If so instructed, it will also print status reports with items categorized by department, and sales control reports for on-hand and reordered items.

The Payroll module prints paychecks, payroll reports, and periodic tax reports. It maintains a record for each employee and updates the record to provide current, quarterly, and year-to-date figures. You can run this package as an independent system, or you can set it up to integrate with the G/L module. If you choose the latter option, current period posting produces a file containing journal entries that transfer automatically to the G/L. The Payroll package prints a transaction register of journal entries to use as an audit trail, or for manual posting to a different ledger.

The module maintains a tax file for calculating federal withholding, FUTA taxes, personal income withholding, and employer's unemployment tax liability. A tax update service, PeachTax, also is available to calculate tax withholding for local entities within a state.

Other features found in the Payroll module include weekly, biweekly, semimonthly, and monthly pay periods; printed paychecks itemizing earning and deduction on the stub; payroll registers; deduction registers; payroll summaries; hours/earnings reports; and a paymaster's worksheet for recording nonstandard earnings or deductions unique to the current pay period.

One minor drawback to the Peachtree system is the format of the screen displays. When you bring up an employee file, for example, there's so much information there, it's hard to get oriented. Peachtree, however, claims this is an attribute, since all the information you could possibly need is right there in one screenful—if you can find it. Menus and input forms also are overcrowded with information, making selections and data entry confusing during the startup phase.

Another minor concern is that some users will find end-of-period processing somewhat tedious. A number of activities occur at the same time, and if a single function fails or is interrupted, some confusion can occur.

The rich functionality and consistent design of the Peachtree Business Accounting System make up for its deficiencies. Easy procedures and routines will decrease learning time for the computer novice, thereby reducing the amount of money you'll have to spend on overtime wages and temporary help. Many businesses, especially those with multifaceted invoicing requirements, may find this system most appealing.

RealWorld Accounting System

COMPANY:	RealWorld Corporation
REQUIREMENTS:	PC-DOS or MS-DOS; 128K; two disk drives or hard disk; 132-column printer.
COMPATIBILITY:	Order Entry/Billing; Job Costing; Sales Analysis.
PRICES:	General Ledger ($695); Accounts Receivable ($695); Accounts Payable ($695); Inventory Control ($695); Payroll ($695). Total Price: $3,475.

The RealWorld Accounting System has a long-standing reputation for its workhorse reliability. A scaled-down version of minicomputer software that was first developed nine years ago, RealWorld stayed competitive by adding to and improving its accounting system's considerable stable of features.

RealWorld's system emphasizes error checking and data safety. Each accounting module incorporates a program which, when activated, checks the integrity of all data on file. This program automatically prints a report of any flaws it detects, including those caused by such anathemas as hardware and DOS failures. The system also offers a simple-but-effective backup and restoration routine which saves your data in ASCII format, thereby making it accessible to many database and word processing programs.

RealWorld's security setup gives you a full range of options. You have the choice of a system-wide password, a password for each main menu function, or a password for whatever group of menu functions you select. This user-defined, multilevel security arrangement is particularly suitable for a local area network, or any multiuser environment where restricting certain operators from sensitive data is a good idea.

Each module comes with two full-size notebooks of documentation. A spiral-bound "Getting Started Manual" contains basic installation, data entry, company file, and password information generic to all modules. Explanations of error messages are unusually complete, and the two glossaries—one of accounting terms, the other of computer terms—total a very generous 50 pages.

The looseleaf "User Manual" also contains a liberal amount of orientation material, including a large quantity of sample data for performing the supplied practice exercises. Though the documentation as a whole is fairly comprehensive, the "Getting Started Manual" claims that all you need to use RealWorld is a "basic knowledge of bookkeeping" (and, presumably, the system's documentation) is a little too optimistic. The lack of an index and the absence of step-by-step instructions for converting from a manual to an automated accounting system make this contention seem all the more dubious.

The G/L module supports a 13-month accounting year that includes budget amounts for each period. Account numbers may be up to seven digits long, the last three digits of which are preceded by a hyphen and designate the account's departmental classification. If you do not opt for departmental accounting, you are left with a four-digit account number—rather skimpy for some businesses.

The G/L program offers simple and straightforward transaction entry, in addition to a number of useful pre-posting features. Transaction listings may be printed for editing in entry order or account number order, and you can generate a working trial balance listing for making adjustments. The regular trial balance listing allows nine levels of subtotals, a choice of any specified date range, and the option to print trial balances for any or all accounts. You may omit detail transactions on the trial balance report so that only summary figures are shown for each account.

RealWorld supports a file for recurring journal entries, and each transaction therein may be assigned either a fixed amount that the program posts automatically, or an amount that you can vary from period to period before posting. General journal entries can be prepared so they are reversed automatically in the next period. When you post transactions to the G/L, the system automatically prints a standard journal transaction register.

RealWorld does not provide a custom report generator. However, the system does include a very flexible formatting program to control the layout of financial statements. The General Ledger generates the familiar balance sheet and profit and loss statement, as well as a variety of statements reflecting cash flow, components of working capital, and changes in financial position.

The Accounts Receivable module centers around the customer file, which maintains account balance, last payment, sales volume, and gross profit history information on each customer. You have the option of at least 36 payment terms, and your selection is represented by the number you decide to enter into each customer record. Basic name and address information is maintained for all customers except one-time patrons, whom you may designate as "miscellaneous," thereby allowing you to bypass regular account setup procedures.

Sales transactions, credit and debit memos, cash receipts, and adjustments are all easily entered and edited. You can post finance charges automatically on the basis of associated dollar amounts, invoice age, a minimum finance charge amount, and two different percentages.

The A/R module supports both open item and balance forward accounting, and the package gives you the option of generating statements according to various billing cycles, including weekly, semimonthly, or monthly on any specified day—rare flexibility in an A/R package. The system also can track sales commissions, and you can print a special commission due report at any time.

The Accounts Payable module automatically assigns voucher numbers to every payable entered, be it a credit, an adjustment, or a prepaid invoice. The system also calculates the due date, discount amount, and discount date at the time of transaction entry, based upon the terms stored in the vendor record. These figures are presented as default values open for editing.

You may enter virtually any payment control information you wish into the A/P package. Discounts, for example, may be subtracted automatically from payment, and vouchers can be paid partially or deferred entirely. Before printing checks, you have the option of printing a precheck writing report for verification. The package automatically prints a check register after the checks are written, thereby providing an audit trail.

The Inventory Control module is a basic reseller's inventory package. You may determine costing on the basis of weighted average, standard, LIFO, or FIFO methods, and you can track stock movement from multiple warehouses. Transaction processing supports the entry and editing of receipts, sales, credits for returns, stock transfers, and adjustments. You may alter the price of inventory items by adding a dollar amount or percentage to the former price of the item, or the cost of the item.

Each item record contains two costs, an item number, a sales history, and an item description, as well as discount, commission, and stock control codes. The Inventory Control package prints a useful selection of reports, including those dealing with purchasing advice, item stock status, inventory valuation, physical count, and A-B-C (high-medium-low usage) analysis.

The Payroll package handles both hourly and salaried employees for daily, weekly, biweekly, semimonthly, and quarterly pay periods. The employee file includes information pertaining to hire and review dates, vacation and sick pay, as well as the standard deduction categories. A provision for deducting union dues allows a fixed rate per hour or a percentage of gross wages.

Multiple states, counties, and local tax tables are user-definable, and you may calculate taxes on a fixed amount of pay for selected employees. End-of-period tax reporting information is produced on reports that can be used as worksheets to complete the required government forms. You can enter handwritten payroll checks into the system, and the package can update quarter-to-date and year-to-date totals automatically.

The RealWorld Accounting System may not be full of bells and whistles, but it is responsive and dependable. Most operations react quickly to commands, although some menu functions do require several long seconds to load—an annoying flaw if you press an incorrect menu selection. However, the system is quick and easy to install, and the various input verification routines should satisfy the most fastidious user. This system has benefitted substantially from its long product history, and contains enough sophisticated features to enhance the efficiency and profitability of a wide range of businesses.

State of the Art

COMPANY:	State of the Art, Inc.
REQUIREMENTS:	PC-DOS, MS-DOS, or CP/M; 128K; two disk drives or hard disk; 80-column printer.
COMPATIBILITY:	Budget & Financial Reporting; Professional Time & Billing; Sales Invoicing; Spreadsheet Connection; The Bookkeeping System.
PRICES:	General Ledger ($595); Accounts Receivable ($595); Accounts Payable ($595); Inventory Control ($595); Payroll ($595). Total Price: $2,975.

The State of the Art integrated accounting series is a very responsive system written in PASCAL. A straightforward menu arrangement clearly identifies all functions and features, making the system a pleasure to use. Screen formatting is clean and concise. Most users only require a little practice before they feel comfortable with this system.

A careful audit trail is maintained by the system in the form of special reports. These reports list transaction journals that allow you to trace any individual transaction back to its source, including those derived from other modules.

Through the Budget and Financial Reporting module, which is sold separately from the G/L program, you have an extensive interface to the outside world. You can dress up and personalize reports through an add-on word processing program, and the compatible spreadsheet program gives you the option of superior budgeting and financial projections.

The editing system throughout State of the Art is quite limited. Deleting the character to the left via the back space key is the only editing function; mistakes made during data entry are corrected by re-entering data into the same field. Cursor and function keys are supported, and the use of control keys is not necessary. If you omit decimal points, the system will place them for you.

Error messages are displayed on the screen with a short explanation of the problem. Most operational errors are avoided by the error-checking system, which validates account numbers and dates as they are entered.

State of the Art's unique manuals are bound in three-ring binders that open up to provide their own stand. The pages are printed on one side only and are meant to be used in flip-chart style.

Each manual contains two main sections, entitled "Getting Started" and "Systems Operations," which introduce you to all aspects of program operations. A useful quick reference guide can be removed from the manual and kept in a convenient location to assist program operation. An index is not included, making the manual difficult to use as an instant reference. Some worksheets are provided for collecting information for operator entry, but if you are going to use a complete information collections system, you have to create some of the required forms.

A special section on accounting theory explains some module operations from an accounting perspective, and a step-by-step guide assists in converting from a manual to a computerized bookkeeping system. A few basic steps have been left out, however, which could lead to some confusion and necessitate an extensive use of the phone support program. The program requires a $50 annual registration fee, plus approximately $1 per minute. You pay for the call.

The General Ledger module will support 13-month accounting. Recurring charges may be set up for automatic entry and posting at user-defined intervals. A full line of account reports is available from the reports menu. It includes the chart of accounts, trial balance, general ledger detail listing, balance sheet, income/expense statement, journal listings, and budget reports. Account activity can be viewed using a special graph showing periods by dollar amount for an individual account or for a range of accounts. The graph also may be printed.

Comparative statements are not available since information from the previous accounting year is not maintained. Budget information is not supported, which limits the reporting ability of the system.

The Accounts Receivable module supports a number of special features for controlling customer accounts. Divisions are supported for cost or profit center accounts, and customers may be handled in balance forward or open item fashion. Tax status codes are supported for classifying state, county, and local tax exemptions, and for calculating tax percentages to be charged. A flexible system for service charges is provided that breaks out amounts over a user-defined number of days, service charges on previous charges, and minimum services included for billing. You can also post service charges to the A/R ledger.

Customer account activity can be reported by a number of different schedules. Customers can be listed in account order or by a special sort order, and reports can include names, addresses, terms, date of last activity, month-to-date and year-to-date sales, and outstanding balances. A salesperson commission report lists sales and commission, and reports can be expanded to include each salesperson's address. Customer information can be omitted entirely from salesperson reports.

The sales tax reporting system automatically allows you to produce reports on a state, county, or local level. The range of sales tax codes is determined when you install the system.

The Accounts Payable module is set up very logically and is easy to use. Once you have set up the vendor file and the files that support it (i.e., G/L category, division file, bank code file, and terms code file), you can enter vendor invoices and prepare them for payment.

Upon command, you may figure invoice amounts and due dates, discount amounts and due dates, and distribute invoice amounts to the proper G/L accounts. In addition, the module automatically selects invoices for payment and produces checks.

The A/P program automatically keeps totals of vendor purchases, returns-to-date, amounts paid, and outstanding balances. It also permits sophisticated reporting that can help you analyze cash flow, vendor patterns, and discount effectiveness, which can be a great help in vendor negotiations.

The A/P module integrates with the G/L module to permit direct payables posting to the G/L. This includes a feature for default G/L distribution on a vendor-by-vendor basis. Other State of the Art applications, such as Check Reconciliation and Job Cost, may be linked to the A/P module, creating a fully integrated accounting system.

Once you establish your inventory master file, supporting files, and enter the beginning balances for each item in your inventory, you can use the transaction posting feature in the Inventory Control module to record all inventory movement. Any movement is quickly recorded as one of four types of transactions: a sale or issue, a purchase order, a receiving report, or an adjustment.

All transactions are verified for accuracy by an automatically printed transaction journal. Once verified, the transactions are updated to the permanent detail file, and the perpetual inventory totals in the master file are adjusted accordingly.

The Inventory Control module allows you to check instantly the status of an item by simply entering the item number. Information that is tracked and updated automatically, as well as information you have stored for later reference (i.e., minimum quantity, economic order quantity, physical locations of items in the warehouse), can be accessed quickly and easily.

An extensive reporting system permits you to produce valuable reports including detailed price lists, reorder requests, inventory turnover reports, and inventory valuation by any one of three costing methods.

The physical inventory system feature of the module is used to freeze the perpetual inventory, produce the physical count sheets by item location, and adjust the perpetual inventory based on the physical count. Since the inventory is frozen internally by the system, you can continue the distribution of goods without interruption.

The State of the Art Payroll module is designed to meet the payroll production and reporting requirements of any small business. Once the system's supporting files have been established, the package can be used to quickly process large amounts of payroll information.

All federal and state tax calculation formulae are already included in the system, and are used to figure appropriate taxes for each employee. In addition, the tax calculation may be altered to meet changes in tax law, and local tax calculation can be added if necessary.

When a payroll is produced, the system displays and calculates all earnings and deductions, using either present employee information (i.e., pay rates, standard number of hours worked, voluntary deduction, and taxes) or additional payroll information, manually entered, for individual employees. Once you've entered all payroll information, the system produces detailed audit reports that ensure the accuracy of all data before checks are printed.

When all data is confirmed, payroll checks are produced detailing all earnings, deductions, and tax information for the period. Summarized gross wages and net earnings for the year-to-date are displayed.

A payroll check register is produced after check printing as a second audit tool before updating the permanent files. Once the payroll data is updated to the files, the system may be used to generate sophisticated analysis reports and forms, including quarterly and yearly government reporting.

In addition to the application packages discussed above, State of the Art offers a low-end, stand-alone product called the Bookkeeping System. The Bookkeeping System offers automation for small cash basis companies whose accounting requirements may not include the extensive features found in the main software line. If you start with the Bookkeeping System and later need additional modules, the data files can be expanded and used with the complete line of integrated accounting packages, thereby offering a logical path to a full-function system.

TCS Total Accounting System

COMPANY:	TCS Software, Inc.
REQUIREMENTS:	PC-DOS, MS-DOS, or CP/M; 128K; two disk drives or hard disk; 132-column printer or 80-column printer with compressed mode.
COMPATIBILITY:	Materials; Sales; Assets; Q*Link; Q*Net; Q*Word; Q*Label.
PRICES:	Ledger ($595); Receivables ($795); Payables ($595); Inventory ($795); Payroll ($595). Total price: $3,375.

The TCS Total Accounting System offers a comprehensive and efficient method of computerized accounting. The system is fully integrated, so information entered in one module will affect other modules as requested. The modules' data structures are maintained by a built-in database manager called TCS QUICK. QUICK allows the system to interface with other products offered by TCS.

A report generator called Simple allows you to create totally customized reports designed to fit your business's requirements. Simple is part of every module supplied by TCS, and it contains useful functions for file manipulation, such as converting ASCII files to or from the database format.

TCS allows you to set up a single password to get into the system. Transaction registers and control reports provide full auditability. Account numbers are verified at the time of entry, and dates also are checked for validity.

The TCS user manuals are thorough and informative. A tutorial section provides step-by-step examples with a detailed discussion of each step, and another section provides the necessary information for successful installation of the software. Backup procedures are covered and the necessary disk labels supplied. Cluttered page formats and no index, however, make specific information hard to find.

The TCS (General) Ledger module collects and maintains G/L transactional information necessary to produce a wide variety of financial reports. Ledger also interfaces with a TCS word processing program, called Q*Word, allowing you to extract information directly from accounting files and generate customized letters, labels, and mailing lists.

TCS Ledger has a master file for creating and maintaining a chart of accounts, a transaction file for recording journal entries, and a temporary transaction file for initial transaction batch entry and editing. The chart of accounts lists the current balance of each account as well as year-to-date, budget, and previous-year amounts. The accounts contained in the master file can be queried, updated, changed, or deleted throughout the master file maintenance program.

Temporary transaction files are used for initial entry of transactions, and for balancing and editing transactions after entry. As long as transactions remain in this file, they can be edited or deleted. Financial statements generated by Ledger include a balance sheet, an income statement, a budget variance report, and an income spreadsheet.

The TCS Receivables module lets you maintain detailed records on all of your customers, and generate invoices, statements, and an array of management reports. Customer files maintain various information, such as alternate shipping addresses, automatic billing amounts, credit limits, multiple pricing levels, and discount and finance charge rates. TCS Receivables records the date and amount of each customer's last invoice, payment, and year-to-date sales. Balance forward and open item accounts also are supported.

An invoice generator produces invoices either on plain paper or pre-printed forms. The program handles discount amounts or percentages and verifies credit limits before and after you enter invoices. The system provides an optional automatic assignment of invoice numbers.

The open credit reconciliation feature includes several options. You may apply credit directly to a particular invoice or to the oldest invoice first, and you can apply credit from selected order numbers or from all open credits. You also can specify whether to apply specific credit amounts, or all credit available.

A query system gives you instant access to current transactions for any customer account. This information may be viewed on the display monitor or subsequently printed out. Statements can be printed for all customers or a range of customers, and include account details or summaries. Other reports assist with sales tax tracking and account aging.

TCS Payables module lets you keep track of both current and aged accounts payable. The system maintains a complete record for each vendor, and helps determine which vouchers to pay by due date, by discount date, or vis-a-vis certain cash requirements. Payables also compiles information which can be updated automatically, including year-to-date purchases and payments, current balances, and date and amount of last check issued.

Invoice information handled by the system includes the invoice date and amount, discount date and terms, and due date. Several reports help you decide which vendors to pay and when. They are: the open voucher report, the cash requirements report, and the aged payable report. After analyzing these reports and considering the amount of cash available, you can make an informed selection of the best vendors and vouchers to pay.

Checks and advices may be printed by the system. After check printing is complete, a check register may be generated listing check numbers and vouchers paid. An end-of-period processing program accumulates the

G/L transactions to be posted. If you are using TCS Ledger, you can make transferral of this information automatic.

The TCS Inventory package tracks the movement of all items in your physical inventory. You can separate this data by product division, product line, profit center, department, item location, and vendor. Current inventory levels are maintained on an item-by-item basis. A worksheet is provided to take physical inventory and enter the results into the system.

A history function lets you select whether to keep a detailed or summary history of inventory status and movements. The history file can store information for up to 12 months. In addition, several different methods for item tracking are provided. You can track by product division, by product line, by serial number, or by lot number.

A wide range of reports are available. They include inventory detail, status and catalog reports, inventory history reports, item tracking reports, as well as reserve, on-order, and reorder reports. The TCS Inventory system can be interfaced with the G/L and A/R modules, as well as the optional Sales and Materials modules.

TCS Payroll allows a company to prepare its periodic payroll for hourly, salaried, and commissioned employees, while accumulating the necessary information for tax reporting. It generates monthly, quarterly, and annual returns to be filed with local, state, and federal governments.

The Payroll package also prepares employees' W-2s and maintains up-to-date information for each employee. The system includes tables for federal withholding and FICA, as well as withholding tables for all 50 states and up to 20 localities from precomputed or user-generated tables. The system automatically produces payroll checks.

TCS Payroll stores each employee's name and address, social security number, pay type, and pay period, plus a monthly, quarterly, and year-to-date record of an employee's pay and deductions. The system uses these records to calculate payroll— including all deductions for each employee— and to print checks, reports, and government forms.

The overall performance of the TCS Total Accounting System is quite good. Screen management has been designed carefully for easy-to-follow operation, and built-in database functions provide excellent response to user input. Learning to use the TCS system to its fullest capacity, however, requires significant time and dedication.

Chapter 6

Comparing Accounting Systems

This chapter contains a series of comprehensive tables which will allow you to compare, point by point, the accounting system software products reviewed throughout this book. The information found in these charts will provide you with the answer you'll need in order to complete the Needs Assessment Checklist in Chapter 3.

Full explanations of the various program features and functions are presented in earlier chapters. For fast and concise definitions, you may want to consult the Glossary or the Index.

- Table 6-1: Basic Information

- Table 6-2: Documentation

- Table 6-3: Global Features

- Table 6-4: General Ledger Features

- Table 6-5: Accounts Receivable Features

- Table 6-6: Accounts Payable Features

- Table 6-7: Inventory Control Features

- Table 6-8: Payroll Features

TABLE 6-1: BASIC INFORMATION

PROGRAM	List Price						
	General Ledger	Accounts Receivable	Accounts Payable	Inventory Control	Payroll	Total	
THE ACCOUNTING PARTNER II	*	*	*	*	*	$ 995	
BPI ACCOUNTING SERIES	$595	$595	$595	$795	$595	$3,175	
CHAMPION BUSINESS ACCOUNTING SOFTWARE	$595	$595	$595	$595	$595	$2,975	
CYMA GENERAL BUSINESS SYSTEM	$795	$795	$795	$795	$795	$2,995	
EASYBUSINESS SYSTEMS	$595	$595	$595	$595	$745	$3,125	
HARDISK ACCOUNTING SERIES	$595	$595	$595	$595	$595	$2,975	
IBM BUSINESS MANAGEMENT SERIES	$695	$695	$695	$695	$695	$3,475	
OPEN SYSTEMS ACCOUNTING SOFTWARE	$695	$695	$695	$695	$695	$3,475	
PEACHTREE BUSINESS ACCOUNTING SYSTEM	$595	$595	$595	$595	$595	$2,975	
REALWORLD ACCOUNTING SYSTEM	$695	$695	$695	$695	$695	$3,475	
STATE OF THE ART	$595	$595	$595	$595	$595	$2,975	
TCS TOTAL ACCOUNTING SYSTEM	$595	$795	$595	$795	$595	$3,375	

*Modules not sold separately.

TABLE 6-1 (Continued)

Operating System	Minimum Memory (RAM) For PC/MS-DOS	Hard Disk Required	Multiuser System	Demo Disk	PROGRAM
PC-DOS, MS-DOS, CP/M-86	128K	No	No	Yes	THE ACCOUNTING PARTNER II
PC-DOS, MS-DOS, CP/M	256K	No	No	Yes	BPI ACCOUNTING SERIES
PC-DOS, MS-DOS, CP/M, CP/M-86	128K	No	No	Yes	CHAMPION BUSINESS ACCOUNTING SOFTWARE
PC-DOS, MS-DOS, CP/M, CP/M-86, MP/M, MP/M-86	64K	No	Yes	Yes	CYMA GENERAL BUSINESS SYSTEM
PC-DOS, MS-DOS	128K	No	Yes	Yes	EASYBUSINESS SYSTEMS
PC-DOS	128K	Yes	Yes	Yes	HARDISK ACCOUNTING SERIES
PC-DOS	256K	Yes	No	Yes	IBM BUSINESS MANAGEMENT SERIES
PC-DOS, MS-DOS, CP/M, MP/M	128K	Yes	Yes	Yes	OPEN SYSTEMS ACCOUNTING SOFTWARE
PC-DOS, MS-DOS, CP/M	128K	No	No	No	PEACHTREE BUSINESS ACCOUNTING SYSTEM
PC-DOS, MS-DOS, CP/M, CP/M-86, MP/M, MP/M-86	128K	No	Yes	Yes	REALWORLD ACCOUNTING SYSTEM
UCSD p-SYSTEM	128K	No	Yes	Yes	STATE OF THE ART
PC-DOS, MS-DOS, CP/M	128K	No	Yes	Yes	TCS TOTAL ACCOUNTING SYSTEM

TABLE 6-1 (Continued)

PROGRAM	Phone Support	Support Terms	
THE ACCOUNTING PARTNER II	213/538-2511†	$50/90 days	
BPI ACCOUNTING SERIES	800/531-5252 512/454-2801	90 days free; $50/module per year	
CHAMPION BUSINESS ACCOUNTING SOFTWARE	800/243-2626 303/987-2588	30 days free; $250/5 hours	
CYMA GENERAL BUSINESS SYSTEM	Dealers Only	Not applicable	
EASYBUSINESS SYSTEMS	408/942-0522†	6 months free or $600/6 modules per year‡	
HARDISK ACCOUNTING SERIES	800/345-3276 701/201-0550	30 days free; $15/call or $350 per year	
IBM BUSINESS MANAGEMENT SERIES	800/426-2266 305/998-2000	$225 per year plus $40 per problem	
OPEN SYSTEMS ACCOUNTING SOFTWARE	612/870-3515	$195/module per year or $1.95 per minute	
PEACHTREE BUSINESS ACCOUNTING SYSTEM	800/554-8900 404/239-3000	90 days free; $146/module per year	
REALWORLD ACCOUNTING SYSTEM	603/798-5700	$200/module per year	
STATE OF THE ART	714/850-0111	$50 fee (1st call free); $20/20 min.	
TCS TOTAL ACCOUNTING SYSTEM	800/835-8943 713/771-6000	30 days free; $300 per year	

†Toll-free number given with paid subscription
‡Includes discounts on vendor products and other benefits

TABLE 6-2: DOCUMENTATION

Index	Tutorial	Glossary of Error Messages	Glossary of Terms	Disk Tutorial	Reference Card	Help Accessible Anytime	Help Context Sensitive	PROGRAM
No	Yes	Yes	Yes	Yes	No	No	No	THE ACCOUNTING PARTNER II
Yes	Yes	Yes	Yes	Yes	No	No	No	BPI ACCOUNTING SERIES
Yes	Yes	Yes	Yes	Yes	Yes	Yes	Yes	CHAMPION BUSINESS ACCOUNTING SOFTWARE
Yes	No	Yes	No	No	No	Yes	No	CYMA GENERAL BUSINESS SYSTEM
Yes	Yes	Yes	Yes	Yes	Yes	Yes†	Yes†	EASYBUSINESS SYSTEMS
Yes	Yes	Yes	Yes	Yes	No	No	No	HARDISK ACCOUNTING SERIES
Yes	Yes	Yes	Yes	Yes	Yes	Yes	Yes	IBM BUSINESS MANAGEMENT SERIES
Yes	Yes	No	Yes	Yes	Yes	No	No	OPEN SYSTEMS ACCOUNTING SOFTWARE
Yes	Yes	Yes	Yes	No	Yes	Yes	No	PEACHTREE BUSINESS ACCOUNTING SYSTEM
Yes	Yes	No	Yes	Yes	No	No	No	REALWORLD ACCOUNTING SYSTEM
No	Yes	Yes	Yes	No	Yes	No	No	STATE OF THE ART
Yes	No	Yes	Yes	Yes	Yes	No	No	TCS TOTAL ACCOUNTING SYSTEM

*With Q*NET
†With EasyPlus

TABLE 6-3: GLOBAL FEATURES

PROGRAM	Max. Amount Per Transaction	Automatic/Manual Decimal Points	Automatic Date Format	13-Month Accounting	Password Protection	Multilevel Security
THE ACCOUNTING PARTNER II	$ 99,999,999.99	Manual	Yes	Yes	Yes	No
BPI ACCOUNTING SERIES	$999,999,999.99	Automatic	Yes	No	Yes	No
CHAMPION BUSINESS ACCOUNTING SOFTWARE	$ 99,999,999.99	Automatic	Yes	No	Yes	Yes
CYMA GENERAL BUSINESS SYSTEM	$999,999,999.99	Automatic, manual	Yes	Yes	Yes	Yes
EASYBUSINESS SYSTEMS	$ 99,999,999.99	Automatic	Yes	No	No	No
HARDISK ACCOUNTING SERIES	$ 99,999,999.99	Automatic	Yes	No	Yes	Yes
IBM BUSINESS MANAGEMENT SERIES	$999,999,999.99	Automatic, manual	Yes	Yes	Yes	No
OPEN SYSTEMS ACCOUNTING SOFTWARE	$ 99,999,999.99	Automatic	Yes	Yes	Yes	Yes
PEACHTREE BUSINESS ACCOUNTING SYSTEM	$ 99,999,999.99	Automatic	No	No	Yes	Yes
REALWORLD ACCOUNTING SYSTEM	$ 9,999,999.99	Automatic, manual	Yes	Yes	Yes	Yes
STATE OF THE ART	$ 99,999,999.99	Automatic, manual	Yes	Yes	Yes	Yes
TCS TOTAL ACCOUNTING SYSTEM	$ 99,999,999.99	Manual	Yes	No	Yes	Yes*

*With Q*NET

TABLE 6-3 (Continued)

Error Handling						
Automatic Backups	Full Disk Warning	Disk Recovery Procedure	Account Numbers Verification	Error Messages Require Action		PROGRAM
No	No	Yes	Yes	Yes		THE ACCOUNTING PARTNER II
No	Yes	No	Yes	No		BPI ACCOUNTING SERIES
Yes	Yes	Yes	Yes	Yes		CHAMPION BUSINESS ACCOUNTING SOFTWARE
No	No	No	Yes	Yes		CYMA GENERAL BUSINESS SYSTEM
No	Yes	Yes	Yes	Yes		EASYBUSINESS SYSTEMS
Yes	Yes	Yes	Yes	No		HARDISK ACCOUNTING SERIES
Yes	Yes	Yes	Yes	Yes		IBM BUSINESS MANAGEMENT SERIES
Yes	Yes	Yes	Yes	No		OPEN SYSTEMS ACCOUNTING SOFTWARE
No	Yes	Yes	Yes	No		PEACHTREE BUSINESS ACCOUNTING SYSTEM
Yes	Yes	Yes	Yes	Yes		REALWORLD ACCOUNTING SYSTEM
Yes	Yes	Yes	Yes	Yes		STATE OF THE ART
Yes	Yes	Yes	Yes	Yes		TCS TOTAL ACCOUNTING SYSTEM

TABLE 6-4: GENERAL LEDGER FEATURES

PROGRAM	Max. Accounts on Chart of Accounts	Max. Departments	Max. Transactions Per Month	No. of Journals	Recurring Entries
THE ACCOUNTING PARTNER II	Unlimited	99	Unlimited	6	No
BPI ACCOUNTING SERIES	8,000	10	Unlimited	6	Yes
CHAMPION BUSINESS ACCOUNTING SOFTWARE	Unlimited	Unlimited	Unlimited	7	No
CYMA GENERAL BUSINESS SYSTEM	9,999	9,999	32,768	26	Yes
EASYBUSINESS SYSTEMS	Unlimited	Unlimited	Unlimited	10	Yes
HARDISK ACCOUNTING SERIES	2,000	999	999	Unlimited	Yes
IBM BUSINESS MANAGEMENT SERIES	Unlimited	Unlimited	Unlimited	5	Yes
OPEN SYSTEMS ACCOUNTING SOFTWARE	Unlimited	Unlimited	Unlimited	7	Yes
PEACHTREE BUSINESS ACCOUNTING SYSTEM	Unlimited	99	Unlimited	9	Yes
REALWORLD ACCOUNTING SYSTEM	9,999	999	Unlimited	2	Yes
STATE OF THE ART	Unlimited	25	Unlimited	Unlimited	Yes
TCS TOTAL ACCOUNTING SYSTEM	Unlimited	99	Unlimited	9	Yes

TABLE 6-4 (Continued)

Chart of Accounts Listing	Trial Balance Worksheet	Budget Listing	G/L & Journal Listings	G/L Closing Report	Capital Statement	Change in Financial Position		PROGRAM
Yes	Yes	Yes	Yes	Yes	Yes	No		THE ACCOUNTING PARTNER II
Yes	Yes	No	Yes	No	No	No		BPI ACCOUNTING SERIES
Yes	Yes	Yes	Yes	No	No	No		CHAMPION BUSINESS ACCOUNTING SOFTWARE
Yes	Yes	Yes	Yes	No	Yes	Yes		CYMA GENERAL BUSINESS SYSTEM
Yes	Yes	Yes	Yes	Yes	Yes	Yes		EASYBUSINESS SYSTEMS
Yes	Yes	Yes	Yes	Yes	No	Yes		HARDISK ACCOUNTING SERIES
Yes	Yes	Yes	Yes	Yes	Yes	Yes		IBM BUSINESS MANAGEMENT SERIES
Yes	Yes	Yes	Yes	Yes	Yes	No		OPEN SYSTEMS ACCOUNTING SOFTWARE
Yes	Yes	Yes	Yes	No	Yes	No		PEACHTREE BUSINESS ACCOUNTING SYSTEM
Yes	Yes	Yes	Yes	Yes	Yes	Yes		REALWORLD ACCOUNTING SYSTEM
Yes	Yes	*	Yes	Yes	*	*		STATE OF THE ART
Yes	Yes	Yes	Yes	No	No	No		TCS TOTAL ACCOUNTING SYSTEM

*With Budget and Financial module

TABLE 6-4 (Continued)

PROGRAM	Listings & Reports						Reports Can Be			Built-in Custom Report Generator
	Balance & Comparative Balance Sheets	Income & Comparative Income Statements	Depreciation & Amortization Schedule	Comparative & Current budget	Budget Variance	Year-to-Date	Quarter-to-Date	Other Period-to-Date		
THE ACCOUNTING PARTNER II	Yes	Yes	No	Yes	Yes	Yes	Yes	Yes	No	
BPI ACCOUNTING SERIES	Yes†	Yes‡	No	No	No	Yes	Yes	Yes	No	
CHAMPION BUSINESS ACCOUNTING SOFTWARE	Yes†	Yes‡	No	||	Yes	Yes	Yes	Yes	No	
CYMA GENERAL BUSINESS SYSTEM	Yes	Yes	No	Yes	Yes	Yes	Yes	Yes	Yes	
EASYBUSINESS SYSTEMS	Yes	Yes	No	Yes	Yes	Yes	Yes	Yes	Yes	
HARDISK ACCOUNTING SERIES	Yes	Yes	No	Yes	Yes	Yes	Yes	Yes	No	
IBM BUSINESS MANAGEMENT SERIES	Yes	Yes	No	Yes	Yes	Yes	Yes	Yes	Yes	
OPEN SYSTEMS ACCOUNTING SOFTWARE	Yes	Yes	§	Yes	No	Yes	No	Yes	Yes	
PEACHTREE BUSINESS ACCOUNTING SYSTEM	Yes	Yes	Yes	Yes	Yes	Yes	No	No	No	
REALWORLD ACCOUNTING SYSTEM	Yes	Yes	No	Yes	Yes	Yes	Yes	Yes	Yes	
STATE OF THE ART	*	*	No	Yes	Yes	Yes	Yes	Yes	No	
TCS TOTAL ACCOUNTING SYSTEM	Yes	Yes	Yes	Yes	Yes	Yes	Yes	Yes	Yes	

*With Budget and Financial module
†Balance Sheet only
‡Income Statement only
§With Fixed Asset module
||Current Budget only

TABLE 6-5: ACCOUNTS RECEIVABLE FEATURES

Max. Customers	Max. Transactions Per Month	Max. Departments	Open Item	Balance Forward	Contract Receivable Accounts	PROGRAM
Unlimited	Unlimited	99	Yes	Yes	Yes	THE ACCOUNTING PARTNER II
4,000	600	10	Yes	Yes	Yes	BPI ACCOUNTING SERIES
Unlimited	Unlimited	999	Yes	Yes	No	CHAMPION BUSINESS ACCOUNTING SOFTWARE
32,768	32,768	9,999	Yes	Yes	Yes	CYMA GENERAL BUSINESS SYSTEM
Unlimited	Unlimited	Unlimited	Yes	Yes	No	EASYBUSINESS SYSTEMS
3,000	999	999	Yes	Yes	Yes	HARDISK ACCOUNTING SERIES
Unlimited	Unlimited	Unlimited	Yes	Yes	Yes	IBM BUSINESS MANAGEMENT SERIES
Unlimited	Unlimited	Unlimited	Yes	Yes	No	OPEN SYSTEMS ACCOUNTING SOFTWARE
Unlimited	Unlimited	99	Yes	Yes	No	PEACHTREE BUSINESS ACCOUNTING SYSTEM
9,999	Unlimited	999	Yes	Yes	No	REALWORLD ACCOUNTING SYSTEM
Unlimited	Unlimited	Unlimited	Yes	Yes	*	STATE OF THE ART
Unlimited	Unlimited	99	Yes	Yes	Yes	TCS TOTAL ACCOUNTING SYSTEM

*Requires Sales Invoicing module

TABLE 6-5 (Continued)

PROGRAM	Recurring Charges	Optional Order Entry Module	Customer Data					
			Credit Limit	Terms Net Days	Percent Discount	Dollar Amount Discount	Salesperson Code	
THE ACCOUNTING PARTNER II	Yes	No	Yes	Yes	Yes	Yes	Yes	
BPI ACCOUNTING SERIES	Yes	Yes	No	No	Yes	No	No	
CHAMPION BUSINESS ACCOUNTING SOFTWARE	No	†	Yes	Yes	Yes	Yes	Yes	
CYMA GENERAL BUSINESS SYSTEM	Yes	‡	Yes	Yes	No	Yes	Yes	
EASYBUSINESS SYSTEMS	Yes	Yes	Yes	Yes	Yes	Yes	Yes	
HARDISK ACCOUNTING SERIES	Yes	No	Yes	Yes	Yes	Yes	Yes	
IBM BUSINESS MANAGEMENT SERIES	No	Yes	Yes	Yes	Yes	Yes	No	
OPEN SYSTEMS ACCOUNTING SOFTWARE	No	Yes	Yes	Yes	Yes	Yes	Yes	
PEACHTREE BUSINESS ACCOUNTING SYSTEM	No	‡	Yes	Yes	No	No	Yes	
REALWORLD ACCOUNTING SYSTEM	Yes	Yes	Yes	Yes	Yes	Yes	Yes	
STATE OF THE ART	No	Yes	Yes	Yes	Yes	Yes	Yes	
TCS TOTAL ACCOUNTING SYSTEM	Yes	Yes	Yes	No	Yes	Yes	Yes	

†Included in A/R module
‡Order Entry in Inventory

TABLE 6-5 (Continued)

Debit/Credit Memos	Automatically Posts Finance Charges	Will Pay Oldest Invoice 1st	Customer Status by Account No.	Customer Status by Invoice No.	PROGRAM
Processing Data			Query System		
Yes	Yes	Yes	Yes	No	THE ACCOUNTING PARTNER II
Yes	Yes	No	Yes	Yes	BPI ACCOUNTING SERIES
Yes	Yes	Yes	Yes	Yes	CHAMPION BUSINESS ACCOUNTING SOFTWARE
Yes	Yes	Yes	Yes	Yes	CYMA GENERAL BUSINESS SYSTEM
Yes	Yes	Yes	Yes	Yes	EASYBUSINESS SYSTEMS
Yes	Yes	Yes	Yes	No	HARDISK ACCOUNTING SERIES
Yes	Yes	Yes	Yes	Yes	IBM BUSINESS MANAGEMENT SERIES
Yes	Yes	Yes	Yes	No	OPEN SYSTEMS ACCOUNTING SOFTWARE
Yes	Yes	Yes	Yes	No	PEACHTREE BUSINESS ACCOUNTING SYSTEM
Yes	Yes	Yes	Yes	Yes	REALWORLD ACCOUNTING SYSTEM
Yes	Yes	Yes	Yes	No	STATE OF THE ART
Yes	Yes	Yes	Yes	No	TCS TOTAL ACCOUNTING SYSTEM

TABLE 6-5 (Continued)

PROGRAM	Alphabetical Customer Listing	G/L Consolidation & Listing	Statements	Sales Summary Report	Commission by Salesperson	Detail Aged Trial Balance	Custom Formats	Letters & Labels
THE ACCOUNTING PARTNER II	Yes	Yes	Yes	Yes	Yes	No	No	No
BPI ACCOUNTING SERIES	Yes	Yes	Yes	No	No	Yes	No	Yes
CHAMPION BUSINESS ACCOUNTING SOFTWARE	§	Yes	Yes	Yes	Yes	No	Yes	Yes
CYMA GENERAL BUSINESS SYSTEM	Yes	Yes	Yes	No	Yes	Yes	No	Yes
EASYBUSINESS SYSTEMS	Yes	Yes	Yes	Yes	||	No	Yes	Yes
HARDISK ACCOUNTING SERIES	Yes	Yes	Yes	Yes	Yes	Yes	No	#
IBM BUSINESS MANAGEMENT SERIES	No	Yes	Yes	Yes	Yes	No	No	No
OPEN SYSTEMS ACCOUNTING SOFTWARE	Yes	Yes	Yes	Yes	Yes	Yes	Yes	Yes
PEACHTREE BUSINESS ACCOUNTING SYSTEM	Yes	Yes	Yes	Yes	Yes	No	No	No
REALWORLD ACCOUNTING SYSTEM	Yes	Yes	Yes	Yes	No	Yes	No	No
STATE OF THE ART	Yes	Yes	Yes	Yes	*	Yes	No	Yes
TCS TOTAL ACCOUNTING SYSTEM	Yes	Yes	Yes	Yes	No	Yes	No	Yes**

*Requires Sales Invoicing module
§With Report Writer module
\|\|In Inventory module
#Labels only
**With Q*LABEL, Q*WORD

TABLE 6-6: ACCOUNTS PAYABLE FEATURES

Max. Vendors	Max. Transactions Per Month	Max. Departments	Open Item	Balance Forward	Contract Payable Accounts	PROGRAM
Unlimited	Unlimited	99	No	Yes	Yes	THE ACCOUNTING PARTNER II
4,000	Unlimited	10	Yes	Yes	Yes	BPI ACCOUNTING SERIES
Unlimited	Unlimited	9,999,999	Yes	Yes	No	CHAMPION BUSINESS ACCOUNTING SOFTWARE
32,768	32,768	9,999	Yes	Yes	Yes	CYMA GENERAL BUSINESS SYSTEM
Unlimited	Unlimited	Unlimited	Yes	Yes	Yes	EASYBUSINESS SYSTEMS
3,000	999	999	Yes	Yes	No	HARDISK ACCOUNTING SERIES
Unlimited	Unlimited	Unlimited	Yes	Yes	No	IBM BUSINESS MANAGEMENT SERIES
Unlimited	Unlimited	Unlimited	Yes	Yes	Yes	OPEN SYSTEMS ACCOUNTING SOFTWARE
Unlimited	Unlimited	99	Yes	Yes	Yes	PEACHTREE BUSINESS ACCOUNTING SYSTEM
9,999	Unlimited	999	Yes	Yes	Yes	REALWORLD ACCOUNTING SYSTEM
Unlimited	Unlimited	Unlimited	Yes	No	No	STATE OF THE ART
Unlimited	Unlimited	99	Yes	Yes	Yes	TCS TOTAL ACCOUNTING SYSTEM

TABLE 6-6 (Continued)

PROGRAM	Vendor Data						Payment Control		
	Terms Net Days	Due Date (Day of Month)	Percentage Discount	Prompt Payment Discount	Contact Person	Pay All Invoices Through (Date)	Manual Check Entry	Payment Date & Starting Check No.	Will Pay Oldest Invoice 1st
THE ACCOUNTING PARTNER II	Yes	Yes	Yes	No	Yes	No	Yes	Yes	Yes
BPI ACCOUNTING SERIES	Yes	Yes	Yes	Yes	No	Yes	Yes	Yes	Yes
CHAMPION BUSINESS ACCOUNTING SOFTWARE	Yes	Yes	Yes	Yes	Yes	Yes	No	Yes	Yes
CYMA GENERAL BUSINESS SYSTEM	Yes	Yes	Yes	Yes	Yes	Yes	No	Yes	Yes
EASYBUSINESS SYSTEMS	Yes	Yes	Yes	Yes	Yes	Yes	Yes	Yes	Yes
HARDISK ACCOUNTING SERIES	Yes	Yes	Yes	Yes	Yes	Yes	Yes	Yes	Yes
IBM BUSINESS MANAGEMENT SERIES	Yes	Yes	Yes	Yes	Yes	Yes	Yes	Yes	Yes
OPEN SYSTEMS ACCOUNTING SOFTWARE	Yes	No	Yes	Yes	Yes	Yes	Yes	Yes	Yes
PEACHTREE BUSINESS ACCOUNTING SYSTEM	Yes	Yes	Yes	Yes	No	Yes	Yes	Yes	Yes
REALWORLD ACCOUNTING SYSTEM	Yes	Yes	Yes	Yes	Yes	Yes	Yes	Yes	Yes
STATE OF THE ART	Yes	Yes	Yes	Yes	Yes	Yes	Yes	Yes	Yes
TCS TOTAL ACCOUNTING SYSTEM	Yes	Yes	Yes	Yes	Yes	Yes	Yes	Yes	Yes

TABLE 6-6 (Continued)

| Query Syst. | | Listings & Reports | | | | | | | |
Vendor Status by Account No.	Vendor Status by Invoice No.	Alphabetical Vendor Listing	Detail Aged Trial Balance	Checks & Advice Printing	Posting Journals	Pre-Check Register	Check Register	Cash Requirements Report	PROGRAM
Yes	No	Yes	Yes	Yes	Yes	Yes	Yes	Yes	THE ACCOUNTING PARTNER II
Yes	Yes	Yes	Yes	Yes	Yes	†	Yes	Yes	BPI ACCOUNTING SERIES
Yes	Yes	*	Yes	Yes	Yes	Yes	No	Yes	CHAMPION BUSINESS ACCOUNTING SOFTWARE
Yes	Yes	Yes	Yes	Yes	Yes	Yes	Yes	Yes	CYMA GENERAL BUSINESS SYSTEM
Yes	Yes	Yes	Yes	Yes	Yes	Yes	Yes	Yes	EASYBUSINESS SYSTEMS
Yes	Yes	Yes	Yes	Yes	Yes	Yes	Yes	Yes	HARDISK ACCOUNTING SERIES
Yes	Yes	Yes	Yes	Yes	Yes	Yes	Yes	Yes	IBM BUSINESS MANAGEMENT SERIES
*	Yes	Yes	Yes	Yes	Yes	Yes	Yes	Yes	OPEN SYSTEMS ACCOUNTING SOFTWARE
Yes	Yes	Yes	No	Yes	No	Yes	Yes	Yes	PEACHTREE BUSINESS ACCOUNTING SYSTEM
Yes	Yes	Yes	Yes	Yes	Yes	Yes	Yes	Yes	REALWORLD ACCOUNTING SYSTEM
Yes	Yes	Yes	Yes	Yes	Yes	Yes	Yes	Yes	STATE OF THE ART
Yes	Yes	Yes	Yes	Yes	Yes	Yes	Yes	Yes	TCS TOTAL ACCOUNTING SYSTEM

*With Report Generator only
†Onscreen only

TABLE 6-6 (Continued)

PROGRAM	Listings & Reports			
	1099 Tax Forms	G/L Consolidation & Listing	User-Defined Aging Periods	Letters & Labels
THE ACCOUNTING PARTNER II	No	Yes	Yes	Yes
BPI ACCOUNTING SERIES	No	Yes	No	Yes
CHAMPION BUSINESS ACCOUNTING SOFTWARE	No	Yes	Yes	*
CYMA GENERAL BUSINESS SYSTEM	No	‡	Yes	No
EASYBUSINESS SYSTEMS	No	Yes	Yes	Yes
HARDISK ACCOUNTING SERIES	No	Yes	Yes	||
IBM BUSINESS MANAGEMENT SERIES	Yes	Yes	Yes	Yes
OPEN SYSTEMS ACCOUNTING SOFTWARE	No	Yes	Yes	Yes
PEACHTREE BUSINESS ACCOUNTING SYSTEM	No	Yes	No	No
REALWORLD ACCOUNTING SYSTEM	No	Yes	Yes	No
STATE OF THE ART	Yes	Yes	Yes	Yes
TCS TOTAL ACCOUNTING SYSTEM	No	Yes	No	§

*With Report Generator only
‡In G/L module only
§With Q*WORD, Q*LABEL
\|\|Labels only

TABLE 6-7: INVENTORY CONTROL FEATURES

Max. Items	Max. Characters in Item No.	Max. Categories	Purchase/Sales Order Systems	Point-of-Sale Interface		PROGRAM
Unlimited	10	Yes	Yes	No		THE ACCOUNTING PARTNER II
8,000	8	99	Yes	No		BPI ACCOUNTING SERIES
Unlimited	10	Yes	Yes	Yes		CHAMPION BUSINESS ACCOUNTING SOFTWARE
32,768	30	1,200	Yes	Yes		CYMA GENERAL BUSINESS SYSTEM
Unlimited	16	1,200	*	No		EASYBUSINESS SYSTEMS
6,000	15	6	No	Yes		HARDISK ACCOUNTING SERIES
Unlimited	15	Unlimited	No	No		IBM BUSINESS MANAGEMENT SERIES
Unlimited	12	1,200	Yes	No		OPEN SYSTEMS ACCOUNTING SOFTWARE
Unlimited	10	999	No	No		PEACHTREE BUSINESS ACCOUNTING SYSTEM
Unlimited	12	999	No	Yes		REALWORLD ACCOUNTING SYSTEM
Unlimited	14	999	No	Yes		STATE OF THE ART
Unlimited	12	99 product lines, 3 product divisions	*	Yes		TCS TOTAL ACCOUNTING SYSTEM

*Sales Order only

TABLE 6-7 (Continued)

PROGRAM	Max. Characters in Description	Quantity on Hand	Unit of Measure	Unit Cost/Price	Quantity Discount	Period-to-Date Units Sold	Quantity on Back Order	Quantity on Purchase Order
THE ACCOUNTING PARTNER II	70	Yes	Yes	Yes	Yes	Yes	Yes	Yes
BPI ACCOUNTING SERIES	15	Yes	Yes	No	Yes	Yes	Yes	Yes
CHAMPION BUSINESS ACCOUNTING SOFTWARE	22	Yes	Yes	Yes	Yes	Yes	Yes	No
CYMA GENERAL BUSINESS SYSTEM	25	Yes	Yes	Yes	No	Yes	Yes	Yes
EASYBUSINESS SYSTEMS	16	Yes	Yes	Yes	Yes	Yes	Yes	Yes
HARDISK ACCOUNTING SERIES	30	Yes	Yes	Yes	Yes	Yes	Yes	Yes
IBM BUSINESS MANAGEMENT SERIES	15	Yes	Yes	Yes	No	Yes	No	Yes
OPEN SYSTEMS ACCOUNTING SOFTWARE	12	Yes	Yes	Yes	Yes	Yes	Yes	Yes
PEACHTREE BUSINESS ACCOUNTING SYSTEM	10	Yes	Yes	Yes	No	Yes	No	No
REALWORLD ACCOUNTING SYSTEM	25	Yes	Yes	Yes	Yes	Yes	Yes	No
STATE OF THE ART	25	Yes	Yes	Yes	No	Yes	No	Yes
TCS TOTAL ACCOUNTING SYSTEM	12	Yes	Yes	Yes	Yes	Yes	No	Yes

TABLE 6-7 (Continued)

Item Data				Processing			PROGRAM
Last Source of Supply	Last Cost	Inventory Location	Inventory Adjustments	Track Sales Order Quantity	Track Purchase Order Quantity	Costing Method	
Yes	Yes	Yes	Yes	Yes	Yes	Moving Average, LIFO, FIFO	THE ACCOUNTING PARTNER II
Yes	Yes	Yes	Yes	No	No	Moving Average, LIFO, FIFO	BPI ACCOUNTING SERIES
Yes	Yes	No	Yes	Yes	Yes	Moving Average	CHAMPION BUSINESS ACCOUNTING SOFTWARE
No	Yes	Yes	Yes	Yes	Yes	Moving Average, LIFO, FIFO	CYMA GENERAL BUSINESS SYSTEM
No	Yes	Yes	Yes	Yes	Yes	Moving Average	EASYBUSINESS SYSTEMS
Yes	Yes	No	Yes	No	No	Moving Average, LIFO, FIFO	HARDISK ACCOUNTING SERIES
No	Yes	Yes	Yes	No	No	Moving Average, Last Cost	IBM BUSINESS MANAGEMENT SERIES
Yes	Yes	Yes	Yes	Yes	Yes	Moving Average, LIFO, FIFO	OPEN SYSTEMS ACCOUNTING SOFTWARE
Yes	Yes	No	Yes	No	No	Moving Average	PEACHTREE BUSINESS ACCOUNTING SYSTEM
No	No	Yes	Yes	Yes	Yes	Moving Average, LIFO, FIFO	REALWORLD ACCOUNTING SYSTEM
No	Yes	Yes	Yes	No	Yes	Moving Average, LIFO, FIFO	STATE OF THE ART
Yes	Yes	Yes	Yes	Yes	Yes	Moving Average, LIFO, FIFO	TCS TOTAL ACCOUNTING SYSTEM

TABLE 6-7 (Continued)

PROGRAM	Listings & Reports								
	Price/Item Status Lists	Slow-Moving Items Report	Stock Transfer Listing	Reorder Report	Under/Over Stock Reports	G/L Consolidation & Listing	Inventory Adjustments Worksheet	Bin/Shelf Labeling	Items by Dollar Volume
THE ACCOUNTING PARTNER II	Yes	No	No	Yes	Yes	Yes	Yes	Yes	No
BPI ACCOUNTING SERIES	Yes	No	No	Yes	No	Yes	Yes	No	No
CHAMPION BUSINESS ACCOUNTING SOFTWARE	Yes	†	No	Yes	Yes	Yes	Yes	Yes	†
CYMA GENERAL BUSINESS SYSTEM	Yes	No	Yes	Yes	Yes	No	No	Yes	No
EASYBUSINESS SYSTEMS	Yes	Yes	Yes	Yes	Yes	Yes	Yes	Yes	Yes
HARDISK ACCOUNTING SERIES	Yes	Yes	No	Yes	Yes	Yes	Yes	No	Yes
IBM BUSINESS MANAGEMENT SERIES	Yes	No	No	Yes	Yes	No	Yes	No	Yes
OPEN SYSTEMS ACCOUNTING SOFTWARE	Yes	Yes	No	Yes	Yes	No	Yes	No	Yes
PEACHTREE BUSINESS ACCOUNTING SYSTEM	Yes	No	No	Yes	No	No	Yes	No	No
REALWORLD ACCOUNTING SYSTEM	Yes	No	Yes	Yes	Yes	Yes	Yes	No	No
STATE OF THE ART	Yes	Yes	Yes	Yes	Yes	No	Yes	No	No
TCS TOTAL ACCOUNTING SYSTEM	Yes	No	No	Yes	Yes	No	Yes	Yes	No

†With Report Generator only

TABLE 6-8: PAYROLL FEATURES

Max. Employees	Cost Accounting	Multilevel Overtime	Special Tax Deductions	Union Withholdings	Bonuses & Commissions	Manual Checks	PROGRAM
Unlimited	No	Yes	Yes	Yes	Yes	Yes	THE ACCOUNTING PARTNER II
6,000	No	Yes	Yes	Yes	Yes	Yes	BPI ACCOUNTING SERIES
Unlimited	Yes	Yes	Yes	Yes	No	No	CHAMPION BUSINESS ACCOUNTING SOFTWARE
32,768	Yes	Yes	Yes	Yes	Yes	Yes	CYMA GENERAL BUSINESS SYSTEM
Unlimited	No	Yes	Yes	Yes	Yes	Yes	EASYBUSINESS SYSTEMS
250	Yes	Yes	Yes	Yes	Yes	Yes	HARDISK ACCOUNTING SERIES
Unlimited	No	Yes	Yes	Yes	Yes	Yes	IBM BUSINESS MANAGEMENT SERIES
Unlimited	Yes	Yes	Yes	No	Yes	Yes	OPEN SYSTEMS ACCOUNTING SOFTWARE
Unlimited	No	No	No	Yes	Yes	Yes	PEACHTREE BUSINESS ACCOUNTING SYSTEM
Unlimited	No	Yes	Yes	Yes	Yes	Yes	REALWORLD ACCOUNTING SYSTEM
Unlimited	Yes	No	Yes	Yes	Yes	Yes	STATE OF THE ART
Unlimited	No	No	No	No	*	Yes	TCS TOTAL ACCOUNTING SYSTEM

*Commissions only

TABLE 6-8 (Continued)

PROGRAM	Mixed Pay Periods	Mixed Wage Types	Shift Differentials Hourly/Percentage	Time Card Entry & Verification	User Entry of Tax Tables	Listings & Reports	
						Summary Statistics	Pay Register
THE ACCOUNTING PARTNER II	Yes	Yes	No	Yes	Yes	Yes	Yes
BPI ACCOUNTING SERIES	Yes	Yes	No	No	No	Yes	Yes
CHAMPION BUSINESS ACCOUNTING SOFTWARE	Yes	Yes	No	Yes	No	Yes	Yes
CYMA GENERAL BUSINESS SYSTEM	Yes	Yes	Yes	Yes	Yes	Yes	Yes
EASYBUSINESS SYSTEMS	Yes	Yes	Yes	Yes	Yes	Yes	Yes
HARDISK ACCOUNTING SERIES	Yes	Yes	No	No	Yes	Yes	Yes
IBM BUSINESS MANAGEMENT SERIES	Yes	Yes	Yes	Yes	Yes	Yes	Yes
OPEN SYSTEMS ACCOUNTING SOFTWARE	Yes	Yes	No	Yes	No	Yes	Yes
PEACHTREE BUSINESS ACCOUNTING SYSTEM	Yes	Yes	Yes	Yes	Yes	Yes	Yes
REALWORLD ACCOUNTING SYSTEM	Yes	Yes	Yes	No	Yes	Yes	No
STATE OF THE ART	Yes	Yes	No	No	Yes	Yes	Yes
TCS TOTAL ACCOUNTING SYSTEM	Yes	Yes	No	No	Yes	Yes	Yes

TABLE 6-8 (Continued)

941s & 940s	W-2s	Deductions Register	Vacation/Sick Time Report	FUTA Report	Tax Tables Listing	G/L Consolidation & Listing	Adjustable Check & Paystub Format	PROGRAM
								Listings & Reports
Yes	Yes	Yes	Yes	Yes	Yes	Yes	No	THE ACCOUNTING PARTNER II
Yes	Yes	Yes	Yes	No	No	Yes	No	BPI ACCOUNTING SERIES
Yes	Yes	No	No	No	Yes	Yes	No	CHAMPION BUSINESS ACCOUNTING SOFTWARE
Yes	Yes	Yes	No	Yes	Yes	†	Yes	CYMA GENERAL BUSINESS SYSTEM
Yes	Yes	Yes	Yes	Yes	Yes	Yes	Yes	EASYBUSINESS SYSTEMS
Yes	Yes	Yes	Yes	Yes	No	Yes	No	HARDISK ACCOUNTING SERIES
No	Yes	Yes	Yes	Yes	Yes	Yes	No	IBM BUSINESS MANAGEMENT SERIES
Yes	Yes	No	Yes	Yes	No	Yes	Yes	OPEN SYSTEMS ACCOUNTING SOFTWARE
Yes	Yes	No	Yes	No	Yes	Yes	No	PEACHTREE BUSINESS ACCOUNTING SYSTEM
Yes	Yes	Yes	Yes	No	Yes	Yes	No	REALWORLD ACCOUNTING SYSTEM
Yes	Yes	No	No	No	Yes	Yes	Yes	STATE OF THE ART
Yes	Yes	No	No	Yes	Yes	Yes	Yes	TCS TOTAL ACCOUNTING SYSTEM

†Located in G/L module

Part III

Accounting Software Resources

Glossary

General Computer Terms

Application software A computer program designed to perform a specific task or function, e.g., word processing, data base management, financial analysis, spreadsheet, etc.

ASCII Acronym for American Standard Code for Information Interchange. A standardized format for encoding characters and functions used by computers. Many word processing programs, for example, read text and data in ASCII format so that they can exchange files with other programs.

Asynchronous communications adapter Used to connect a modem to a computer. This device does not need special timing signals from the computer or host to transfer data. See communications card.

Backup A reserve copy of information in computer memory, retained on tape or disk in the event the original is lost or damaged.

BASIC Acronym for Beginner's All-purpose Symbolic Instruction Code. A high-level computer programming language originally developed at Dartmouth College as an instructional tool. BASIC is the most common language available for microcomputers.

Baud The speed or rate of computer data flow.

Benchmark An historically significant software program that represents a standard against which other programs of the same type or application are measured. Although it may have been a best-seller at one time, a benchmark program may no longer be the "best" in its software category.

Bit Derived from the words "binary digit," this is the most elementary form of data used by a computer. Each bit has a value of either one or zero (1 or 0); a string of eight bits makes one byte.

Boolean operators The logical operators "and," "or," "not," "except," "if," "then," and "else" used separately or in various combinations by a computer program to decide if a statement is true or false or to assist in the retrieval of specific information based on these values; named after the English mathematician, George Boole.

Boot A general term used to describe starting up a microcomputer system.

Byte A single character of data used by a computer. Each byte is comprised of eight bits.

Central processing unit (CPU) Like a switchboard, the main body of a computer where data is controlled (i.e., routed and processed) by means of a system of internal microprocessors.

Character A single letter, number, or symbol representing a byte of binary data. A character can also be a space, tab, or carriage return.

Command A sequence of keystrokes that activates a particular program function.

Communications card Also referred to as a communications adaptor. A plug-in board often required by a central processing unit in order to facilitate the interface between a computer and a modem.

Configure To setup a computer system for a specific purpose, such as compatibility with certain hardware and/or software.

CP/M Acronym for Control Program for Microprocessors. A computer operating system created by Digital Research Corporation for microcomputers with 8-bit CPUs.

CP/M-86 An operating system created by Digital Research Corporation for microcomputers with 16-bit CPUs.

CRT Acronym for cathode ray tube; the picture tube used in a computer display unit.

Cursor An electronic position marker on the video display screen. Cursor location and function is controlled through keyboard or mouse commands.

Data The actual information stored in a field.

Database A structured collection of related information stored in one or more files and serving one or more applications. The database is independent from and should not be confused with the program that actually manipulates the information.

Data disk A blank disk formatted for your computer operating system and used to store your program records. For example, these disks may contain all of your business's accounting records or word processing documents.

Data Interchange Format (DIF) A format for data files that allows the data to be accessed by more than one type of program. DIF was designed to format data for transfer from one program to another by Software Arts, Inc.

Default Refers to a value or an instruction that is automatically accepted by a computer program unless the current operator enters a different instruction.

Disk A general term referring to either a floppy disk or a hard disk. A floppy disk is a flexible magnetic recording medium housed inside a plastic envelope. A hard disk is not flexible or removable, and is housed inside a closed case. Hard disks have a greater storage capacity than floppy disks.

Disk drive A computer memory device that allows fast and accurate positioning within and between data files, operating instructions, and portable and fixed storage media. Disk drives allow entry, updating, and changing of data through read/write operations.

Disk emulator See RAM disk.

Disk operating system (DOS) A collection of programs that controls input, output, and internal management of data in a computer and on disk.

Documentation Instructional material, primarily in written form, that explains the operation of specific software or hardware.

Dot matrix printer A printer that produces characters made up of arrays of dots. These printers are faster and less expensive than letter quality printers.

Double density A disk drive system that keeps twice as much information in the same space as a single-density system. Also used to refer to a disk that has information stored on it via a double-density disk drive system.

Double sided A disk drive system in which information can be stored and extracted from both sides of a disk. If, for instance, a single-sided, single-density, 5 1/4-inch disk can hold 90,000 bytes of information (90K), then a double-sided or a double-density disk would hold 180K, and a double-sided, double-density disk would hold 360K.

Download Move information from a central host computer to a smaller unit.

8-bit microprocessor A microprocessor that moves information through the computer in groups of eight bits.

Electronic disk See RAM disk.

Encode The process of electromagnetically writing information onto the magnetic surface of a disk or tape.

Error message A screen indication that a particular error has occurred. For example, "Warning: Disk Full" would indicate that the memory limit has been exceeded.

Error recovery The methods made available by a software program for remedying errors. An irrecoverable error is one that forces loss of data or exit from the program.

External memory Refers to mass storage devices, the most common of which is a magnetic disk drive.

Field An area in a record stored in computer memory which is set aside for a specific type of information.

File A collection of specific information, usually consisting of records, that is stored in a logical fashion.

Floppy disk See disk.

Format To prepare a disk for storing data.

Function key A key that has a special function controlled by the program. Function keys often provide the convenience of pressing one key instead of a series of keys.

Hardcopy Output printed on paper by a computer.

Hard disk A nonremovable data disk sealed inside the computer cabinet; also known as a fixed disk. A hard disk provides large amounts of storage (typically, 10 megabytes) and rapid access.

Hardware The physical components of a computer system, e.g., monitor, keyboard, printer, CPU, etc.

Head A small electromagnet used to read or write information onto the magnetic surface of a tape, disk, or drum.

Input Information that is entered into a computer system.

Interface A connection or common boundary enabling a system or program to acquire information from another system or program; also describes interaction between user and computer.

Kilobyte Abbreviated "K," a kilobyte equals 1,024 bytes of memory.

Justification The adjustment or spacing of character lines to a uniform length at margins.

Letter quality printer A printer that produces characters made up of letter quality letters. These printers are slower and more expensive than dot matrix printers.

Megabyte Abbreviated "M," a megabyte consists of 1,024K or approximately one million bytes of memory.

Memory The data storage areas in a computer. Data stored on microchip is in random access memory (RAM), and is emptied when the computer is turned off. Data stored on tape or on disk is in read only memory (ROM), and remains intact when the computer is turned off.

Menu A screen display listing the commands, options, or selections currently available for execution.

Microchip Also called a chip, a small piece of silicon or other semiconductor that has been etched with a microscopic pattern of circuits. Chips are the building blocks of computer memory.

Microcomputer A small but complete microprocessor-based computer system that can be used by one person at a time.

Microprocessor The microchip that contains a microcomputer's central data processing circuitry.

Mode A condition or status of a program that usually implies readiness to perform a certain kind of task, such as an "editing mode."

Modem A communication device that permits the transfer of data between computers over standard telephone lines.

MS-DOS A disk operating system designed by Microsoft, Inc. MS-DOS ("MS" for Microsoft) is the software's generic name, while PC-DOS is the specific implementation of MS-DOS for the IBM PC.

Multiuser A computer system that can be used by more than one person at the same time.

Operating system The program that controls the most basic operations of the computer. The operating system interfaces application software with computer hardware.

Output Information sent by the computer to a screen, printer, plotter, or storage device.

Parallel port Allows eight bits of data to be transferred back and forth between the computer and a peripheral device such as a printer.

PC-DOS An operating system that is the specific implementation of MS-DOS for the IBM PC.

Peripherals Additional hardware that is connected to the basic computer (e.g., printer, modem, joystick).

Plotter A computer output device that draws figures, diagrams, or other graphics using one or more colored pens.

Port A point in a computer's circuitry designed for data input or output. A printer is connected to a computer via either a parallel or a serial port.

Printer A computer output device that prints characters or graphics on paper.

Program A set of computer instructions, also known as software.

Prompt A symbol or statement that appears onscreen to indicate that a program, a language, or an operating system is ready for use.

RAM disk An electronic disk created with extra Random Access Memory.

Random access A mode of data access where data or blocks of data can be read directly, and in any order. This makes it unnecessary to read all the way from the beginning of a file or block of data to obtain the desired information.

Random access memory (RAM) Memory that allows the user direct access to any storage location; information can be written into or read out of these locations. Also called user memory, RAM is volatile; its contents are lost when power is turned off.

Read-only memory (ROM) Memory in which data is stored permanently. Such memory is nonvolatile, as it is unaffected when power is turned off.

Read/write head See Head.

RS-232 A standard for connecting data processing and data communications hardware (i.e., computers, terminals, printers, plotters, modems, etc.) with serial interfaces, established by the Electronic Industries Association in 1969.

Screen Same as CRT, video display, or monitor.

Serial port Transfers one bit of data back and forth between the computer and a peripheral device such as a printer.

Single density A disk drive system that has a space capacity, which is half as much as a double-density disk drive system, in the same amount of space.

Single sided A disk drive system that only reads or writes data on one side of a disk, as compared with double-sided disk drives.

16-bit microprocessor A microprocessor that moves information through the computer in groups of 16 bits.

Smart modem A modem that is controlled by the user from the computer instead of through switches on the modem itself.

Software Information and instructions that direct computers to perform specified tasks, as opposed to the electronic devices (hardware) which execute them. All computer programs are software.

Spreadsheet The electronic version of an accountant's worksheet, represented on a video display by a grid of cells referenced by row and column coordinates. Spreadsheets often contain many built-in formulae and functions used in financial modeling and numeric recalculation.

UCSD p-System A disk operating system that operates as a kind of universal translator. The p-System was developed by the University of California at San Diego (UCSD) and is usually packaged with one or more programming languages.

Utilities Programs that perform routine operations, e.g., data integrity checks or file sharing.

Accounting Software Terms

940 Form A federal reporting form listing the amount of federal tax withheld from an employee's payroll, and an employer's and employee's contribution to FICA. This form is filed quarterly.

941 Form A federal reporting form listing the amount of federal unemployment tax contributed by the employer. This form is filed yearly.

942 Form A household employee who receives a W2 is reported on a 942 form rather than a 941 form.

1099 Form A federal reporting form listing the amount of money paid to a contractor who is not subject to withheld taxes.

Account file The file holding the general ledger chart of accounts.

Account number An abbreviated code used to identify an account. The account number used in an automated accounting system is usually six characters long.

Accountability When money is loaned or when people invest in a business, it's the duty of that business to account for the use of the money.

Accountant Someone who examines the financial data of a business, and advises the owner on where the business stands financially.

Accounting equation Assets = Liabilities + Equity.

Accounting period The period of time a business chooses to calculate its financial position. This is usually a calendar month, but it may be every four weeks, or any specified interval.

Accounting principle A rule that guides the accounting and activities of a business.

Accounting system A system required to provide management with information needed for planning, controlling, and reporting the financial conditions and operations of a business.

Accounts payable Monies owed to vendors for goods or services.

Accounts payable account A liability account representing the balance of all invoices, payments, and adjustments posted for vendors.

Accounts receivable Monies owed to a company for goods and services rendered.

Accrual basis A system of recording transactions as they occur. Income and expenses are recognized and recorded as incurred, regardless of whether money was actually received or paid during that period.

Accrued expense An expense that is unpaid by the end of a given period.

Accrued revenue Revenue earned during an accounting period that is not received by the end of a given period.

Accumulated depreciation The total depreciation that has collected to date for one asset account.

Adjustments Changes made in business accounts. Adjustments are usually made to accounts for returns, bad debts, and depreciation, and are a necessary reflection of the changing financial position of a company.

Aging A method used to establish the age of a transaction for processing and listing. Aging is performed according to the system date or a date entered by the operator prior to processing.

Aging accounts receivable A process where an aged trial balance is prepared listing each customer's balance with its corresponding age.

Alphanumeric A set of characters consisting of either letters of the alphabet (A-Z), digits (0-9), special symbols, or any combination thereof. For example, PG-50 is an alphanumeric expression.

Amortization The procedure followed in allocating the cost of long-lived assets to the periods in which their benefits are derived. For fixed assets the amortization is called depreciation expense.

Application program A type of software that provides the user with the functions necessary to perform a group of related tasks. General ledger, accounts receivable, accounts payable, payroll, and inventory programs may be referred to as application programs.

Assets The property or resources that a business owns.

Audit report A report detailing what is in a given file at a particular moment.

Audit trail A record of transactions that allows you to trace an account balance through time to the source of individual transactions.

Average cost A method of inventory valuation that determines a dollar amount by weighted average; dividing the total cost of inventory by the total number of units on hand.

Average daily balance A calculation method used to determine the portion of an account due on a daily basis. The amount may be used to calculate a service charge to be applied to an overdue account.

Average time to pay A calculation method used to predict the amount of time between sending a statement and receiving a customer payment.

Balance forward The sum total of an account carried forward into the next accounting period after end-of-month processing. Accounting detail is not included in the balance forward method.

Balance sheet Reflects the financial position of a business by summing its assets and liabilities, to arrive at an equity figure. The balance sheet indicates the solvency of a company.

Batch A collection of related transactions prior to posting.

Batch processing Related transactions gathered into groups for processing into a ledger.

Billing cycle The period of time for which billing statements are issued. While it is usually monthly, the billing cycle is ultimately determined by the individual requirements of a company.

Book value The net amount of an asset shown in the accounts of a firm. When referring to an entire firm, it relates the excess of total assets over total liabilities (also referred to as owner's equity or net worth).

Bookkeeping The record-making phase of accounting.

Budgeting Planned financial activities of an enterprise compared with its actual financial performance.

Capital The total assets of a firm; may also be the owner's equity.

Capital account An account used to record the equity of an owner's business.

Cash accounting An accounting method in which income and expenses are recognized as such when monies actually change hands, rather than when income is earned or expenses incurred.

Cash disbursements The paying of invoices or monies due.

Cash flow The excess or deficiency of cash receipts over cash disbursements for a given period.

Chart of accounts A list of all accounts that a business maintains in its general ledger.

Check register A listing that contains entries for recording payments by check.

Chronological listing Transaction items ordered by date.

Company profile The general characteristics of a company that you enter into an application program, e.g., the amount of interest a company charges on overdue accounts. Information entered in a company profile will have global effects throughout the program.

Control account A general ledger account that summarizes the total of a subsidiary ledger—e.g, the month's receipts from a cash fund in accounts receivable.

Cost accounting The process of calculating the amount of money required to manufacture a product, or to provide a service or portion of a service.

Cost of goods sold The total cost allocated to the production of a completed product for a particular period.

Costing of inventory A phrase describing the valuation of current inventory. Different costing methods will have different effects when calculating cost of goods sold.

Credit terms The payment arrangement agreed upon by a customer who already has taken possession of goods from a vendor.

Current assets Assets that are either presently in the form of cash, or can be converted into cash within a short time period.

Current liabilities Payments due within a short time period.

Customer Someone buying goods or services from your business. The main record in accounts receivable is the customer record.

Customer code The identifying abbreviation assigned to a particular customer; used to reference that customer's transactions.

Customer file The file containing basic information on each customer in the accounts receivable system.

Debit An increase in liabilities, expenses, taxes, and dividends; a decrease in retained profits, assets, revenues, share capital, and reserves.

Default (accounting) Failure to pay an account.

Defer To postpone payment on a voucher.

Department A subdivision of a company.

Depreciation An asset's yearly reduction in value due to physical wear and tear or to functional obsolescence.

Detail file A file containing all posted transactions and their descriptions.

Discount A deduction from the retail price of goods, usually contingent on payment within a specified period of time.

Discount date The date that payment must be made in order to obtain a prearranged reduced price.

Distribution The distribution of credits and debits to the general ledger accounts.

Distribution accounting The allocation of transactions to the departments from which they originated.

Double entry system The basic accounting procedure that maintains equality in the accounting equation by recording equal credit and debit amounts.

Edit list A listing of transactions from a work file that is printed before posting to check for accuracy.

Employee code The identifying abbreviation assigned to an employee for payroll transaction functions.

Employee file The data file containing payroll information for employees.

End-of-period processing Procedures performed at the end of an accounting cycle, which may include posting accounts, printing reports, consolidating accounts, purging satisfied transactions, and backing up data.

End-of-year posting Procedures performed at the end of a fiscal year, which may include purging satisfied transactions, posting accounts, printing reports, consolidating accounts, backing up data, and bringing forward account balances to start the new fiscal year.

Ending balance The balance of an account at the end of an accounting cycle.

Entry Any transaction entered into the accounting system.

Equity The rights or claims to the assets of a business.

Expense A cost absorbed by a business in an attempt to obtain revenue.

Extended cost An amount that appears on a purchase order and is equal to the unit cost of the item times the number of items being ordered.

Extended price An amount that appears on an invoice; equal to the list price of the item times the number of items being sold.

Federal Insurance Contributions Act (FICA) A tax paid by employees and matched by the employer on wages earned up to a specified amount; Social Security tax.

Federal Unemployment Tax (FUTA) A tax paid by employers on wages up to a specified amount.

Financial accounting The accurate recording of the assets and liabilities of a business.

Financial reporting The primary output activity of an automated accounting system, usually performed by the general ledger. Financial reporting often allows you to custom format your accounting information on reports.

First in, first out (FIFO) A method of determining the value of inventory based on the selling of oldest inventory items first.

Fiscal period One of the accounting periods of a company's business or fiscal year; usually a calendar month.

General accounting The accounting work of recording transactions and preparing financial statements.

General journal Journal containing transactions that cannot be allocated to other subsidiary journals.

General ledger One of the four ledgers in the double entry system used to record transactions, including assets, liabilities, revenue, and expenses.

Gross profit Net sales minus cost of goods sold.

Income Revenues realized from sales or services.

Income statement A financial statement that shows revenues earned, the expenses incurred in earning those revenues, and the resulting net income or net loss.

Input screen An electronic version of a paper business form, in which you enter the details of a particular transaction or master file record. Input screens are comprised of fields designed to hold specific items of information.

Integrated accounting software An automated accounting system consisting of separate program modules that can share the same files or file structures.

Interest Monies charged to overdue accounts receivable. Also, monies paid for the use of capital and due in addition to repayment of that capital.

Inventory A detailed list of items in stock.

Invoice A list that itemizes goods sold, their price, and terms of sale.

Item code The identifying abbreviation assigned to an inventory item; used as a reference to transactions involving that particular item.

Item file The file containing basic information on each item in the inventory control system.

Journal A means of grouping financial activity by source to simplify the audit trail.

Key security A security method that uses a specially coded disk to control access to a computerized accounting system.

Last in, first out (LIFO) A method of determining the value of inventory based on the concept of selling the most recent inventory items first.

Lead time The amount of time between placing an order and the receipt of goods.

Ledger A collection of accounts used by a business in recording its transactions.

Liability The financial obligations entered in the balance sheet.

Line item A single entry that represents any quantity of an inventory item.

Listings Basic auditing and editing documents (hardcopy) printed out by an accounting module in fixed format.

Management accounting Information derived from a financial statement that assists in making decisions about the business. Examples: How much does it cost to manufacture a product? Should the business invest in more equipment? Should the business raise the price of the product?

Master File A file within an accounting module that contains the accounts to which transactions are posted.

Net income The amount by which total expenses are exceeded by total revenues for a given period.

Net loss The amount by which total revenues are exceeded by total expenses for a given period.

Normal posting The assignment of transactions to their designated accounts.

Open item A method of account handling that itemizes all unpaid transaction detail.

Order entry A program to record and process sales transactions. Order entry may interface with accounts receivable and inventory control programs.

Owner's equity The net balance of total assets minus liabilities.

Password protection A security system that relies on a key word or code number to restrict access to all or part of an automated accounting system.

Pay period A fixed time period that determines how often an employee receives wages. Weekly, monthly, semimonthly, and biweekly are common pay periods.

Pay types The method by which an employee receives wages. Hourly, salary, and commission are common pay types.

Payroll The system that maintains and processes information regarding payment of a company's employees.

Point-of-sale A phrase describing the point in a retail business when money actually changes hands, i.e., at the cash register. Some inventory accounts receivable systems provide elaborate point-of-sale tracking capabilities.

Posting The process of permanently affixing transactions to the correct ledger accounts.

Procedural error A mistake in transaction processing characterized by an improper sequence of operations—e.g., purging transaction files before printing an audit trail.

Profit center A department or division of a business that incurs costs and generates revenues.

Program disk The disk containing the programs that make up an accounting software module. Many accounting modules are made up of several program disks.

Purchase order A request to a vendor for goods or services.

Purging A function that frees disk space for storage. Purging should be conducted after listings and postings are completed during the accounting cycle.

Query system An information retrieval system that allows you quick, onscreen access to accounting records.

Realization principle The accounting maxim that defines revenue as an inflow of assets. Revenue must be recognized as such at the time it is earned.

Record A collection of information for an individual account. For example, each account record in accounts receivable contains the customer code, name, address, terms, etc.

Recurring batches Collections of transactions that occur on a monthly basis, stored in a special file for automatic posting to designated accounts.

Recurring charges Monthly charges automatically posted to designated customer accounts in accounts receivable.

Reports Your main hardcopy source of information (as opposed to listings) concerning the financial state of your business. Reports from an automated accounting system may be in either fixed or user-defined format, and include such documents as profit and loss statements, balance sheets, and comparative statements.

Retained earnings Profits that are not paid out to shareholders, but kept in the business.

Revenue The gross increase in a company's equity as a result of profitable business transactions.

Reversing entry An entry that reverses the adjusting entry for an item.

Revolving charge account A type of balance forward account that consolidates invoicing detail into an outstanding balance, and calculates the amount due for each period according to the terms established for a customers account.

Sinking fund A fund accumulated to pay off a public or corporate debt.

Special posting Assigning transactions from the previous year to an account.

Subsidiary accounts A group of accounts with a common characteristic.

Subsidiary ledger Collection of accounts other than the general ledger accounts that detail the transactions resulting in the balance of a general ledger account.

Suspense account An account that accumulates amounts that will be disbursed or distributed at a later time. Careful use of suspense accounts can provide cash type accounting within an accrual accounting system. See also sinking fund.

System error A serious error caused by a computer hardware malfunction, often resulting in a loss of data.

Tax file A data file containing tax rates or schedules used as a reference during program operation; also known as tax tables.

Tips-deemed-wages Unaccounted-for wages that are automatically taxed five percent by employers.

Transaction An entry into one of the accounting modules detailing a date, a reference number, a description, and a credit or debit amount.

Transaction files The main storage area for transaction information, purged by the system at the end of an accounting period. A hardcopy of transaction file contents provides the primary audit trail in a computerized system.

Transaction processing The entry, distribution, and storage of transaction information.

Trial balance A list of all open accounts having balances in a given ledger.

Vendor code An identifying abbreviation assigned to a vendor and used to reference transactions involving that vendor.

Vendor file The file containing basic information on each vendor in the accounts payable system.

Voucher A record of an accounts payable transaction.

W-2 form A federal reporting form that lists an employee's wages paid for the year and his or her deductions by category.

Weighted average A method of costing inventory by dividing the total number of inventory items into the total cost of all items; also called moving average.

Year-to-date file A general ledger file which holds a detailed record of all transactions for the fiscal year.

Appendix A

Evaluation and Review Criteria

This evaluation form has been designed by ONE POINT to be used by all accounting software product reviewers. The questions concern both objective and subjective information about the program to be reviewed. A space for additional comments also is provided at the end of the booklet.

Contents

1. General Product Information

2. Documentation

3. Ease of Learning and Ease of Use

4. Global Parameters, Editor, Error Handling

5. Software Review and Evaluation
   A. General Ledger
   B. Accounts Receivable
   C. Accounts Payable
   D. Inventory Control
   E. Payroll

6. Special Features and Functions

7. Support, Service and Maintenance

8. Synopsis

General Product Information

Product name:

Publisher:

Address:

Telephone:

Price per module:
   General Ledger: $
   Accounts Receivable: $
   Accounts Payable: $
   Inventory Control: $
   Payroll: $
   Other modules: $

Total list price: $

Evaluator's System Configuration:

Machine used:

Operating system:

Memory (K):

Number of disk drives:

Add-on circuit boards:

Peripherals:

System and Hardware Requirements:

1. Machines supported:

2. Operating systems supported:

3. Minimum memory required (K):

4. Recommended (K):

5. Add-on circuit boards required
   (e.g., printer card, graphics card):

6. Requires: ☐ 132- ☐ 80-col. printer

7. Printers supported:

8. Requires: ☐ Mono ☐ Color monitor

9. Monitors supported:

10. Other peripherals supported:

11. Programming language:

12. Method of indexing/sorting:

13. Other software required
    (e.g., interpreters, runtime modules):

14. Multiuser configuration (if supported):

15. Compatible software:

Documentation

1. Operations manual includes:
   ☐ Table of contents ☐ Index
   ☐ Registration card ☐ Tabs
   ☐ Bibliography ☐ Glossary
   ☐ Sample exercises ☐ Tutorial
   ☐ Quick reference card

☐ Error message appendix
☐ Forms for manual data collection
Total pages:

2. Binding:
   ☐ Spiral ☐ Looseleaf ☐ Hard
   ☐ Slip case ☐ Other (specify):

3. Print:
   ☐ Typeset ☐ Dot matrix
   ☐ Photocopied ☐ Other (specify):
   ☐ Print color(s):
   ☐ Frequent typos?

4. Illustrations:
   ☐ Menus ☐ Other displays
   ☐ Printouts ☐ Flow charts
   ☐ Other (specify):

5. Date of publication: Last revision:

6. Rate discussion of setup and installation:
   ☐ Excellent ☐ Below average
   ☐ Good ☐ Poor
   ☐ Average ☐ Not included
   Are installation procedures provided
   for specific microcomputer systems?

7. Rate the documentation as a user
   reference tool:
   ☐ Excellent ☐ Below average
   ☐ Good ☐ Poor
   ☐ Average

8. Rate the overall clarity of the
   documentation:
   ☐ Excellent ☐ Below average
   ☐ Good ☐ Poor
   ☐ Average

9. Rate explanations and examples of
   functions and commands:
   ☐ Excellent ☐ Below average
   ☐ Good ☐ Poor
   ☐ Average ☐ Not included

10. Rate organization of documentation:
    ☐ Excellent ☐ Below average
    ☐ Good ☐ Poor
    ☐ Average

11. Rate usefulness of user tutorials:
    ☐ Excellent ☐ Below average
    ☐ Good ☐ Poor
    ☐ Average ☐ Not included

12. Rate usefulness of index:
    ☐ Excellent ☐ Below average
    ☐ Good ☐ Poor
    ☐ Average ☐ Not included

Ease of Learning and Ease of Use

1. Rate ease of installation:
   ☐ Easy ☐ Average ☐ Difficult

2. Rate the online tutorial:

□ Excellent □ Below average
□ Good □ Poor
□ Average □ Not included

Accessible at any time?

3. Sample applications disk:
   No. of applications:
   Type of applications:

4. Rate demo disk:
   □ Excellent □ Below average
   □ Good □ Poor
   □ Average □ Not included

5. Additional training available from:
   Books: Software:
   Other:

6. Est. time to learn basic functions:
   □ Less than 1 day □ 3 to 4 weeks
   □ 1 to 6 days □ Over 4 weeks
   □ 1 to 2 weeks □ Still learning

7. Command may be entered in:
   □ English □ Abbreviated form

8. Usefulness of onscreen error messages:
   □ Excellent □ Below average
   □ Good □ Poor
   □ Average □ Not included

9. The program is:
   □ Menu driven □ Command driven
   □ Tree structured □ Web structured

10. Menus are:
    □ Optional □ Fixed □ Nonexistent

11. Online help is:
    □ Context-sensitive □ Nonexistent
    □ Accessible at any time □ Multilevel

12. What is most difficult aspect(s) of program to learn and use?

13. What features/functions are well-designed for the new user?

14. Features you would add or change:

15. Rate overall ease-of-use of software pkg.:
    □ Very easy □ Difficult
    □ Easy □ Impossible
    □ Fair

General Features

1. Security
   □ Password(s) □ Multilevel

2. File handling
   Will share among modules:
   □ Company profile
   □ Vendor list □ Customer list
   □ Reads/writes ASCII files
   □ Reads/writes DIF files
   □ Automatic file backups

3. Error handling
   □ "Full disk" warning
   □ File recovery procedure
   □ Acct. nos. verified at time of entry
   □ Onscreen backup reminder
   □ Error messages require action

4. Rate usefulness of error messages:
   □ Excellent □ Below average
   □ Good □ Poor
   □ Average □ Not included

5. Data handling
   □ Automatic EOP processing
   □ Maintains/tracks historical data
   □ Prior period posting
   □ Special period posting
   □ 13-month acct. □ Batch processing
   □ Automatic decimal points
   □ Automatic date formatting
   □ Recurring entries □ Reverses entries
   Max. dollar amount per transaction:
   Max. total dollar amount:

6. Rate difficulty of changing basic setup information:
   □ Very easy □ Difficult
   □ Easy □ Impossible
   □ Fair

7. Editing
   □ Cursor keys supported
   □ Function keys supported
   □ Delete character right
   □ Delete character left
   □ Insert mode □ Insert character
   □ Erase field □ Erase to end of line
   □ Previous field □ Next field

Software Review and Evaluation

A. General Ledger

1. Multiple companies supported □

2. Auto. integration w/ subsidiary ledgers □

3. Chart of accts.
   No. of accts.: No. of depts.:

4. Acct. types
   □ Balance sheet □ Income
   □ Retained earnings
   □ Alphanumeric acct. nos.
   Max. characters for acct. no.:

5. Acct. information maintained
   □ Current monthly history
   □ Previous year monthly history
   □ Budget system for current yr by acct
   □ Current balance □ Opening balance

6. Transaction information
   Max/no. of transactions:
   Max/no. of journals:
   □ Account no. □ Dept. no.

☐ Date ☐ Source journal
☐ Reference no. ☐ Description
☐ Amount ☐ Debit or credit
☐ Period

7. Processing
   ☐ Batch processing
   ☐ 13-month accounting
   ☐ Recurring entries
   ☐ Reversing entries
   ☐ External batch input

8. Query ability
   ☐ View accts. ☐ View budget amts.
   ☐ Show transactions onscreen
   ☐ View current year periods
   ☐ View previous year periods

9. Formatted listings
   ☐ Comp. profile ☐ Chart of accts.
   ☐ Trial balance worksheet
   ☐ Budget listing ☐ G/L listing
   ☐ Batch status report
   ☐ Journal listings ☐ Batch listings
   ☐ G/L ledger closing report

10. Formatted reports
    ☐ Capital stmt. ☐ Balance sheet
    ☐ Change in financial position
    ☐ Income stmt. ☐ Budget report
    ☐ Comparative balance sheet
    ☐ Comparative income statement

11. Depreciation & amortization schedule
    ☐ Straightline ☐ Declining balance
    ☐ Sum of years digits

12. Posting
    ☐ Automatic posting ☐ Special posting
    ☐ Prior period posting

13. Accounting control
    ☐ Complete audit trail
    ☐ Account # & journal # verification
    ☐ Force balanced entries

14. Report generator
    Report length (if limited): # of col.:
    ☐ Flexible report periods
    ☐ Cover pg. & notes for financial stmt.
    ☐ Subtotals at any point (by group)
    ☐ Zero balance acct. suppression
    ☐ Control of signs ☐ Auto. rounding
    ☐ Print control (underlining, bold, etc.)
    ☐ Col. ctrl. ☐ Acct. consolidation

16. Acct. calculation
    ☐ Between different accts.
    ☐ Columns expressed as math functions

17. Perform following tasks & comment:
    Set up a new acct.:
    Post transactions to an acct.:
    Generate a financial report:

18. Comment on speed of operation:

B. Accounts Receivable

1. Invoicing
   # of customers: # of transactions:
   # of depts.: Customer code size:
   ☐ Open item and/or balance forward
   ☐ Contract receivable accts.

2. Offers optional order entry system

3. Customer information:
   ☐ Name ☐ Address
   ☐ Phone ☐ Credit limit
   ☐ Terms net days, % on amt. over
   ☐ Disc. by % ☐ Disc. by $ amt.
   ☐ Salesperson code
   ☐ YTD purchases ☐ YTD payments
   ☐ Date last invoice ☐ Amt. last invoice
   ☐ Date last payment ☐ Amt. last payment

4. Invoice information:
   ☐ Invoice no. ☐ Reference no.
   ☐ Description ☐ Date
   ☐ Amount ☐ G/L distribution

5. Payment entry:
   ☐ Automatic payment against oldest
     invoice first

6. Query system:
   ☐ Customer status lookup by acct. code
   ☐ Global system lookup by range of custs.
   ☐ Transaction details viewed onscreen

7. Other processing operations:
   ☐ Posting of recurring charges
   ☐ Separate audit trail for cash sales
   ☐ Posting of finance charges

8. Fixed Reports:
   ☐ Alphabetical listing of customers
   ☐ Summary statistics report
   ☐ Detail aged trial balance
   ☐ Summary aged trial balance
   ☐ Statements
     If yes, custom formats available?
   ☐ Letters/labels ☐ Merge with WP
   ☐ Invoice posting journal
   ☐ Invoice journal ☐ Payment journal
   ☐ Adjustments journal
   ☐ Cash sales jrnl ☐ Cash posting jrnl
   ☐ Adjustments posting journal
   ☐ Add/credit memos ☐ Sales sum. rpt.
   ☐ Commission reports by salesman
   ☐ G/L consolidation and listing

9. Benchmark test:
   No. of customers in sample files:
   Time required to post transactions:

10. Comment on any operations that seem
    to be sluggish or slow:

11. Perform the following steps and com-
    ment on the general ease of use:
    ☐ Enter a new customer

☐ Enter an invoice ☐ Post invoice
☐ Enter a payment ☐ Post payment
☐ Perform EOM processing to include generation of a statement
☐ Consolidate monthly transactions and post to G/L

C. Accounts Payable

1. Does the system have an interactive purchase order system available?
   # of vendors: # of transactions:
   # of depts.:   Vendor code size:
   ☐ Open item and/or balance forward
   ☐ Contract payable accts.

2. Vendor information:
   ☐ Name   ☐ Address
   ☐ Phone   ☐ Due date
   ☐ Terms net days, % on amount over
   ☐ Disc. by %   ☐ Contact
   ☐ YTD purchases   ☐ YTD payments
   ☐ Date last invoice ☐ Amt. last invoice
   ☐ Date last payment ☐ Amt. last payment

3. Invoice information:
   ☐ Invoice no.   ☐ Reference no.
   ☐ Description   ☐ Date
   ☐ Amount   ☐ G/L distribution

4. Payment control entry:
   ☐ Automatic payment against oldest invoice first
   ☐ Pay all invoice up through (date)
   ☐ Manual check entry
   ☐ Specification of payment date & starting check no.

5. Query system:
   ☐ Vendor status lookup by acct. no.
   ☐ Global system lookup by range of vendors
   ☐ Transaction details viewed onscreen

6. Fixed reports:
   ☐ Alphabetical listing of vendors
   ☐ Summary statistics report
   ☐ Variable aging periods
   ☐ Detail aged trial balance
   ☐ Summary aged trial balance
   ☐ Checks and advices?
      If yes, custom formats available?
   ☐ Letters/labels ☐ Merge with WP
   ☐ Invoice posting jrnl ☐ Invoice jrnl
   ☐ Adjustments journal
   ☐ Pre-check register ☐ Check register
   ☐ Cash requirements report?
      If yes, report periods variable?
   ☐ 1099 forms ☐ Adj. posting jrnl
   ☐ G/L consolidation & listing

7. Benchmark test:
   No. of vendors in sample data base:
   Time required to post ___ transactions:

8. Comment on any operations that seem to be sluggish or slow.

9. Perform the following steps and comment on the general ease of use:
   Enter a new vendor:
   Enter an invoice for the vendor:
   Perform a check run to pay the vendor:
   Perform end-of-month processing to purge the complete transaction:
   Perform G/L consolidation to see the effect of the transaction in the G/L:

D. Inventory Control

1. General:
   ☐ Interactive to P/O and S/O system
   ☐ Point-of-sale interface
   ☐ Facility for tracking serial no.s
   Max/no. of items:
   No. of characters in item #:
   ☐ Segments are allowed within item #

2. Items:
   ☐ Item no.   ☐ Item description
   ☐ Quantity   ☐ Qty. on hand
   ☐ Unit of measure ☐ Unit cost
   ☐ Unit price   ☐ Qty. discount
   ☐ MTD units sold ☐ QTD units sold
   ☐ YTD units sold ☐ Sales dollars
   ☐ Cost of goods sold ☐ Category
   ☐ Order point quantity
   ☐ Qty. back-order ☐ Qty. on P.O.
   ☐ Last vendor   ☐ Last cost
   ☐ Inventory location (bin/shelf)

3. Processing:
   ☐ Physical inventory adjustments
   ☐ Track quantity committed to S.O.
   ☐ Track quantity on P.O.
   ☐ Weighted moving average costing
   ☐ LIFO costing   ☐ FIFO costing

4. Reports:
   ☐ Item summary statistics
   ☐ Price list   ☐ Status list
   ☐ Physical inventory adj. listings
   ☐ Basic sales listing ☐ List. sort by $ vol.
   ☐ Graphic sales analysis
   ☐ Slow-moving items listing
   ☐ Stock transfer listing
   ☐ Bin/shelf labeling ☐ Reorder report
   Others:

5. Additional features module provides:

6. Perform following steps and comment on general ease of use:
   Enter a new item:
   Receive shipment of item:
   Ship item:
   Perform EOP consolidation and transfer to G/L:

E. Payroll

1. Are the following features available:
   - ☐ Provides a U.S. certified payroll
   - ☐ Performs cost accounting
   - ☐ Supports multilevel OT structure
   - ☐ Supports shift diff. hourly or by %
   - ☐ Provides for special tax deductions
   - ☐ Provides local tax withholdings
   - ☐ Tax table support from vendor

2. Setup:
   - ☐ FICA percentage and cut-off limit
   - ☐ SDI percentage and cut-off limit
   - ☐ Entry, edit, and print local, state & federal tax tables
   - ☐ User-defined recurring deductions (fixed amount & cutoff)

3. Employees:
   No. of employees:
   - ☐ Employee code ☐ Name
   - ☐ Dept. code ☐ Address
   - ☐ Phone ☐ Social Security #
   - ☐ Ethnic class. ☐ # of deductions
   - ☐ Pay rate ☐ Pay period

4. Processing:
   Time cards:
   - ☐ Misc. deductions ☐ Bonus
   - ☐ Commissions ☐ Manual checks
   - ☐ Mixed pay periods
   Reports:
   - ☐ Checks & pay stubs (custom formats available)
   - ☐ Summary statistics
   - ☐ Pay register ☐ 941s ☐ W-2s
   - ☐ Special tax reports (DE-3, WR-30, etc)
   - ☐ Time card entry report
   - ☐ Deductions register
   - ☐ Payroll summary ☐ FUTA report
   - ☐ Tax file listings ☐ EOM reports
   - ☐ EOQ reports ☐ EOY reports
   - ☐ G/L consolidation & summary rpt.

5. Benchmark test:
   No. of employees in data base?
   Processing time to calculate payroll?
   Processing time to post payroll?

6. Perform following steps and comment on general ease of use:
   Update a tax table:
   Adjust FICA upper limit and cutoff:
   Enter a new employee:
   Complete pay cycle for new employee to include entering hours worked, generate pay register and print checks:
   Consolidate payroll for the G/L

Special Features and Functions

What features or special capabilities did you find unique to package?

Are there functions within package overlooked by the evaluation instrument?

Support, Service and Maintenance

1. Provided by:
2. 800 no. ☐ Collect ☐ Toll ☐
3. Days of week support available:
4. Hours of day support available:
5. Support terms:
6. Software available for evaluation:
7. Copy protected ☐ If yes, method:
8. Vendor backups available:
9. User expected to make backup copies:
10. Updates available for $_____ free ☐
11. Defective product replacement policy:
12. Update policy:
13. If you tried to obtain assistance from publisher/manufacturer, rate assistance?
    - ☐ Very helpful ☐ Not helpful
    - ☐ Somewhat helpful ☐ Not offered
14. Comments:

Synopsis

1. Overall rating of software:
   - ☐ Excellent ☐ Below average
   - ☐ Good ☐ Poor
   - ☐ Average

2. Please rate the following:
   Ease of general day-to-day use:
   - ☐ Excellent ☐ Below average
   - ☐ Good ☐ Poor
   - ☐ Average
   Ease of special functions:
   - ☐ Excellent ☐ Below average
   - ☐ Good ☐ Poor
   - ☐ Average
   Ease of EOP processing & consolidation:
   - ☐ Excellent ☐ Below average
   - ☐ Good ☐ Poor
   - ☐ Average

3. Recommend software? Why/Why not?

4. Please comment on:
   Distinctive features:
   Suitable applications:
   Possible end users:
   Please add extra comments as needed.

Accounting Software Directory

This directory contains a number of microcomputer accounting software products currently on the market. The listings are intended primarily for business accounting applications.

All software packages are listed alphabetically by product name and are available in versions that will run on IBM Personal Computers or on IBM PC-compatible computers. The first group of products contains all of the accounting programs reviewed in this book. Each listing includes the software publisher's name, mailing address, and telephone number.

The Accounting Partner II
Star Software Systems
20600 Gramercy Place
Torrance, CA 30326
213/538-2511

BPI Accounting Series
BPI Systems, Inc.
3423 Guadalupe
Austin, TX 78731
512/454-2801

Champion Business Accounting Software
Champion Software Corp.
17301 W. Colfax −250
Golden, CO 80401
303/987-2588

CYMA General Business System
CYMA Corp.
2160 Brown Rd.
Mesa, AZ 85203
602/835-8880

EasyBusiness Systems
Sorcim/IUS Micro Software
2195 Fortune Dr.
San Jose, CA 95131
408/942-1727

Hardisk Accounting Series
Great Plains Software
1701 38th St. SW
Fargo, ND 58103
701/281-0550

IBM Business Management Series
IBM Corp.
1000 NW 51st St.
Boca Raton, FL 33432
305/998-2000

Open Systems Accounting Software
Open Systems, Inc.
430 Oak Grove
Minneapolis, MN 55403
612/870-3515

Peachtree Business Accounting System
Peachtree Software, Inc.
3445 Peachtree Rd. NE
Atlanta, GE 30326
404/239-3000

RealWorld Accounting System
RealWorld Corp.
Willow Hill Bldg. Dover Rd.
Chichester, NH 03263
603/798-5700

State of the Art
State of the Art, Inc.
3191-C Airport Loop
Costa Mesa, CA 92626
714/850-0111

TCS Total Accounting System
TCS Software, Inc.
6100 Hillcroft #600
Houston, TX 77081
713/771-6000

The remainder of this directory contains additional accounting software products that may be of interest. Since these programs were not reviewed or evaluated for this book, readers are advised to research them carefully before making a buying decision. Some of the software publishers listed may offer demonstration disks of their programs; for further information, contact the vendors directly.

AMI CPA System
Automation Management, Inc.
5718 Westheimer #410
Houston, TX 77057
713/781-5941

Accountability Retailer
General Accounting-Renaissance
Software Strategies, Inc.
7412 Washington Ave. South
Eden Prairie, MN 55344
612/941-4044

Accounting Pearl
Pearlsoft
P.O. Box 638
Wilsonville, OR 97070
503/682-3636

Advantage One Financial System
Advantage One, Inc.
1142 Willagillespie #12
Eugene, OR 97401
503/485-4022

Attache Commercial Accounting System
The Computer Company
3 Illinois
Chicago, IL 60601
312/938-9133

The Boss Business Software Products
Balcones Computer Corp.
2625 Buell Ave.
Austin, TX 78758
512/346-1771

BIAS
Bristol Information Systems
84 North Main St.
Fall River, MA 02720
617/679-1051

Contract Manager
OB Manager
BBC, Inc.
251 Merill St.
Birmingham, MS 48011
313/645-5280

CP Aims
Gemini Information System
5500 S Syracuse Circle
Englewood, CO 80111
303/773-1805

Desktop Accountant
Rocky Mountain Software Systems
P.O. Box 3282
Walnut Creek, CA 94598
415/680-8378

Easyacct
Miracle Computing
313 Clayton Ct.
Lawrence, KS 66044
913/843-5863

Financial Accounting Package
ABW Corp.
P.O. Box 1047
Ann Arbor, MI 48106
313/971-9364

General Accounting
Groundstar Software
2160 41st Ave.
Capitola, CA 95010
408/462-5250

General Accounting System
Consolidated Computer Group
P.O. Box 5246
Tacoma, WA 98405
206/272-6993

General Ledger
Accounts Receivable
Accounts Payable
Dow Jones & Co., Inc.
P.O. Box 300
Princeton, NJ 08540
609/452-2000

General Ledger II
CP Aids, Inc.
1061 Fraternity Circle
Kent, OH 44240
216/678-9015

Insoft Accountant
Insoft, Inc.
P.O. Box 19208
Portland, OR 97219
503/244-4181

Integrated Company Management
Microcomputer Consultants
P.O. Box 1377
Davis, CA 95617
916/756-8104

The Integrated Billing System
Custom Software, Inc.
15 Mackay Place
Brooklyn, NY 11209
212/748-3153

MBA Accounting Software
Micro Business Applications
12281 S. Nicollet Ave.
Burnsville, MN 55337
800/622-5463

Macola Financial System
Macola, Inc.
P.O. Box 485/181 South Main St.
Marion, OH 43302
614/382-5991

Maxi Accountant
The Business Division
P.O. Box 3435
Longwood, FL 32750
305/862-6917

The Medallion Collection
Timberline Systems, Inc.
P.O. Box 230120
Portland, OR 97223
503/644-8155

Metro Tracker
Metrosoft, Inc.
11333 Iowa Ave.
Los Angeles, CA 90025
213/473-0972

Microbiz
Compumax Associates, Inc.
P.O. Box 7239
Menlo Park, CA 94026
415/854-6700

PASS
Plenary Systems, Inc.
9669 Wendell Rd.
Dallas, TX 75243
214/343-9901

PEP Business System
PEP Engineering
3970 Syme Dr.
Carlsbad, CA 92008
619/434-6023

Pro/Gacc
Pro/Ware
953 Mountain View Dr.
Moraga, CA 94549
415/283-7620

The Profit Center
Prentice-Hall, Inc.
200 Old Tappan Rd.
Old Tappan, NJ 07657
800/526-0485

Small Business Accounting
Small Business Management System
Howe Software
14 Lexington Rd.
New City, NY 10956
914/634-1821

Sybiz Accounting Software
Heritage Software, Inc.
3757 Wilshire Blvd. #211
Los Angeles, CA 90010
213/384-5430

Versa Business
H & E Computronics, Inc.
50 N Pascack Rd.
Spring Valley, NY 10977
914/425-1535

Univair Super Ledger Accounting
Univair, Inc.
9024 St. Charles Rock Rd.
St. Louis, MO 63114
314/426-1099

Appendix C

Bibliography

The following references to articles and books will provide you with further information on accounting software and on many of the specific products mentioned in this book. You also will find several general references to useful materials on computerized accounting systems.

The first section lists relevant articles from a number of well-known periodicals, most of which contain additional reviews on the software products featured in this book. For current or back issues, check local libraries and computer stores, or contact the magazine publisher directly.

The next section contains a list of books which will serve as helpful references in understanding more about computerized accounting, operating microcomputer systems (like the IBM Personal Computer) and accounting software.

Periodicals

Brown, Errol. "Accounting Partner." *Popular Computing,* August 1984, pp. 170-172.

Casella, Philip. "Corporate MBA." *PC Products,* October 1984, pp. 69-71.

Crabb, Don. "BPI General Accounting." *InfoWorld,* March 25, 1985, pp. 43-45.

Crabb, Don. "Accounting Partner II." *InfoWorld,* March 4, 1985, pp. 45-47.

Dalton, Richard. "New Wave Accounting Systems." *Popular Computing,* May 1985, pp. 27 + .

Dauphinais, G. William. "Six Easy Pieces: Accounting Packages from IUS." *PC Magazine,* October 30, 1984, pp. 223-231.

Dauphinais, G. William. "Exploring the Profit Center." *PC Magazine,* October 2, 1984, pp. 195-201.

Dauphinais, G. William. "Inventory Control for Retailers." *PC Magazine,* August 7, 1984, pp. 215, 220-225.

Dauphinais, G. William, and Yesko, Michael A. "Sizing up the Basic Four." *PC Magazine,* October 30, 1984, pp. 234-253.

Dauphinais, G. William, and Yesko, Michael A. "An Attache from Down Under." *PC Magazine,* September 4, 1984, pp. 192-200.

Feakins, Nicholas L. "A Review of the RealWorld Accounting System." *Unix World,* November 5, 1984, pp. 78-83.

Field, Cynthia. "Back to Basics." *InfoWorld,* November 12, 1984, pp. 53-54.

Heintz, Carl. "Automating Your Business Accounting Functions." *IBM PC Update,* December 1984, pp.14-22.

Heintz, Carl. "Buyer's Guide to General Ledger Software." *Interface Age,* July 1983, pp. 70 + .

Guttman, Michael K. "How to Choose an Accounting Package." *PC World,* October 1984, pp. 57-63 + .

Heite, Edward F. "SPI's Open Access." *PC Products,* October 1984, pp. 73-75.

Lints, Delsi. "Champion's Accounting System Keeps Users in Mind." *Computer Software News,* May 21, 1984, pp. 52 + .

Mansfield, Ron. "Finding What You Need in Accounting Software." *Business Software,* December 1984, pp. 26-30.

McCoy, James A. "The Bottom Line On Top-of-the-Line Accounting." *Microcomputing,* January 1984, pp. 78-85.

Miller, Charles A. "Accounting for the IBM/XT." *Personal Software,* July 1984, p. 58.

Monk, Thomas J., and Landis, Kenneth M. "Accounting for a New System." *Business Computer Systems,* December 1984, pp. 29-32.

Post, Dan. "Striking a Balance." *Business Computer Systems,* August 1984, pp. 92-100 + .

Post, Dan. "General Ledger's Bottom Line." *Business Computer Systems,* July 1984, pp. 68-70 + .

The, Lee. "Accounting for Accounting-phobes." *Personal Computing,* November 1984, pp. 291-296.

Whitmore, Sam. "BMS Software from IBM gets Mixed Reviews." *PC Week,* October 9,1984, p.5.

Books

Arnold, David. *Getting Started with the IBM PC and XT.* New York, NY: Simon & Schuster, Inc., 1984.

Davis, Frederic E. *Hardware for the IBM PC and XT.* New York, NY: Simon & Schuster, Inc. 1984.

Freiberger, Stephen, and Chew, Paul. *A Consumer's Guide to Personal Computing and Microcomputers.* Rochelle Park, NJ: 1980.

Frankel, Philip, and Gras, Ann. *The Software Sifter: An Intelligent Shopper's Guide to Buying Computer Software.* New York, NY: Macmillan Publishing Co., 1983.

Fry, Louis, and Adams, Marcia. *The Business Microcomputer Handbook.* New York, NY: Holt, Rinehart and Winston, 1984.

Hockney, Donald. *Personal Computers for the Successful Small Business.* New York, NY: Macmillan Publishing Co., 1984.

Highland, Harold J. *Protecting Your Microcomputer System.* New York, NY: John Wiley & Sons, Inc., 1984.

Hixson, Amanda C. *A Buyer's Guide to Microcomputer Business Software.* Reading, MA: 1984.

Isshiki, Koichiro R. *Small Business Computers: A Guide to Evaluation and Selection.* Englewood Cliffs, NJ: Prentice-Hall, 1982.

Kenney, Donald P. *Personal Computers in Business.* New York, NY: Amacom (American Management Associates), 1985.

Morgan, James, C.P.A. *Computer Power for Your Accounting Firm.* Berkeley, CA: Sybex, Inc., 1984.

Needlman, Theodore. *Microcomputers for Accountants.* Englewood Cliffs, NJ: Prentice-Hall, Inc., 1983.

Page, John, and Hooper, Paul. *Accounting and Information Systems.* Reston, VA: Reston Publishing Co., Inc., 1982.

Tiller, Susan Losey; Parker, John D.; and Halkyard, Edwin M. *An IBM Guide to Choosing Business Software.* Wayne, PA: Banbury Books, 1984.

Trademark Acknowledgments